My Story, His Glory

Samantha Buttle

Dedication

To all those who have endured the weight of pain and trauma, in any shape or form it may have manifested, this heartfelt dedication is for you. May my story serve as a beacon of hope, gently illuminating the path toward healing and restoration. And in the midst of it all, may it lead you to the embrace of the Lord, my savior, who holds the power to mend even the most shattered of souls.

To my beloved children,

This book is dedicated to the three souls who have brought immeasurable joy and purpose into my life. You all are the greatest blessings I could have ever asked for, and each day spent watching you grow and learn fills my heart with indescribable happiness.

The pages of this book offer a testament to the boundless love, unwavering support, and unwavering belief in your potential that I have always held in my heart for you. You have been my inspiration, my motivation, and my reason to strive for love, healing, forgiveness, and peace.

As you navigate through the twists and turns of life, my dear children, may this book serve as a guiding light. No matter where we are going, there's only one way to go from here, and that's up. May its stories, lessons, and experiences shape your character and fuel your dreams. Always remember that you are capable of achieving anything you set your minds to and that my love for you is infinite and everlasting. NOTHING IS IMPOSSIBLE

With profound gratitude and love,

Acknowledgment

First and foremost, I express my heartfelt gratitude to Isabelle. Your encouragement, wisdom, guidance, and understanding fueled this creative journey. You are truly a gift to this world.

A special thanks goes to the dedicated team at Eternal Ghost Writers, who have tirelessly worked behind the scenes to bring this book to life. Your professionalism, expertise, and attention to detail are truly commendable.

To all those who have played a part, big or small, in the creation and publication of this book, I am forever grateful. Your contributions have made this journey a blessing, and I am honored to have worked with you all.

Lastly, my sincere thanks to the readers; your curiosity and engagement make these words come alive. This book is a collective endeavor, and I am deeply thankful for the hands that have touched its pages.

About the Author

After a lifetime filled with pain and suffering and venturing down countless wrong paths, Samantha Buttle emerges as a remarkable author. Her literary works are ablaze with an unwavering commitment to truth, exuding a fiery passion that captivates readers. With each word she writes, she fearlessly confronts her biggest challenges, defying those who have sought to keep her silent and confined.

Gazing into the mirror, Samantha sees her true self and reflects on the journey that led her here. Through self-acceptance and unconditional love, she fearlessly explores the depths of her human experience, embracing her imperfections and navigating the labyrinth of emotions with unwavering courage. Her narrative dismantles the walls that shield vulnerability, fostering a profound understanding that by embracing our authentic selves, we unlock the path to genuine healing and a life lived with authenticity and integrity.

In her own healing, Samantha has discovered her calling, paving the way for a brighter future for others, including her three children. Through her actions, she can only hope she creates small ripples of change, ensuring that those who follow in her footsteps will not endure the same level of adversity she faced. With unwavering confidence, she forges a pathway towards a better tomorrow.

Chapter 1: Haley Station

Growing up in Haley Station, a picturesque small town surrounded by nature, my family seemed perfect to outsiders. However, beneath this idyllic façade, our family life was riddled with emotional coldness, unspoken truths, and the constant pressure to conceal our true selves.

From an outsider's perspective, we seemed like the ideal family. Nestled in the quaint town of Haley Station, our home was situated in the heart of Cottage Country. The breathtaking beauty of our surroundings was undeniable, with nature's splendor enveloping us at every turn. My parents built our house on a generous five-acre plot, which was truly a child's paradise.

Just outside our front door, an expansive wilderness awaited. It beckoned me to explore and run as far and as freely as I wished. Our home was located about two kilometers off the main road, down a dirt path lined with trees that provided shelter and serenity. We were constantly reminded of how fortunate we were to have such a life.

Growing up, I was told that we had everything a child could ever want: a spacious house, well-stocked cupboards, an inground pool, snowmobiles, all the latest gadgets, and branded clothes. It seemed that whatever our hearts desired was within our reach.

At night, the skies above our home would reveal a stunning display of stars and constellations, a testament to the beauty and tranquility of our surroundings. Living in such a picturesque place was truly a blessing. Our family enjoyed vacations to Florida, where my parents owned a timeshare, and we attended church regularly. We spent considerable time with my mother's side of the family during holidays but never with my father's side. Despite residing in such an enchanting place, I find it difficult to recall many happy memories from my childhood. The love, hugs, and care that one would expect in a warm family environment seemed to be missing. Instead, there was an emotional coldness that pervaded our home, and I was often labeled as the "problem child."

Although we seemed like a stable and happy family, appearances can be deceiving. Even today, people might hold misconceptions about our family based on those appearances. We were always taught to hide our true, authentic selves. Embracing our individuality, speaking up for ourselves, and sharing our genuine feelings were considered unacceptable.

Speaking openly about our lives, troubles, and everything happening behind closed doors was strictly forbidden. We were expected to keep our family's issues private and not discuss them with anyone outside our home. I remember how this expectation affected me, particularly when dealing with issues like bullying or conflicts with my brother.

If I ever sought help or reported his behavior, I would be the one who got into trouble. It was as if we were expected to be like light switches, able to turn off our emotions and feelings at a moment's notice. We had to step out of the car, or any situation, for that matter, with a cheerful disposition, as if nothing had ever happened. To this day, I feel as though my parents and brother are still very adept at maintaining this facade. Mornings during my childhood were filled with negativity and tension, making it an incredibly challenging environment to navigate. Even something as simple as deciding how to style my hair or what clothes to wear could result in an argument.

My mother controlled many aspects of my life, from the clothes I wore to the food I ate. Starting each day surrounded by negativity had a significant impact on the rest of my day and, ultimately, on the person I became. Over time, I found myself transforming into a miserable and negative individual.

Behind closed doors, it seemed as though there was an unspoken agreement that nothing was wrong with our family's behavior. I was conditioned to lie and keep up appearances, a skill that took me a long time to unlearn. The constant fear of getting into trouble weighed heavily on my mind. If there was an issue at school and a call had to be made home, I would spend the entire day anxiously anticipating the consequences.

I would agonize over the shame and the guilt punishments awaiting me. The anxiety of the unknown when I returned home was an ever-present burden that took a toll on my emotional well-being.

The emotional strain was immense, and report card days were the worst. I can still vividly recall receiving my report card at school and spending the entire journey home consumed by dread. I would imagine my father sitting in his rocking chair, waiting for us to arrive. He would always open my brother's report card first, praising him and expressing pride in his accomplishments. But then it was my turn, and I can't recall a single instance when my parents told me they were proud of me or acknowledged my achievements. I was raised to avoid making mistakes, but often, I couldn't even tell if something was genuinely a mistake or not. Consequently, I would lie to avoid potential repercussions, even if I had done something positive. Fear of my parents' reactions drove me to deception. In a way, it felt as though I was raised in a bubble, cut off from genuine emotional connections and constantly trying to navigate the uncertain expectations and consequences of my actions. It seemed as if everything I did was wrong, and I was oblivious to the existence of any kind of outside world. I often found solace in solitude, spending countless hours alone in my bedroom, listening to the Backstreet Boys. Writing became my savior, providing an escape from the reality of my difficult childhood.

I would fantasize about the Backstreet Boys rescuing me from my unhappy circumstances, and music became a vital outlet for me. When it came to my schoolwork, I rarely received assistance from my parents, and on the few occasions they did help, it usually ended in arguments and frustration because they couldn't understand the material.

I was always slow to grasp new concepts, if I even managed to grasp them at all. What would be considered a learning disability today was due to constant exposure to traumatic events. Those events had a massive effect on my attention, memory, and cognition. Being stuck in survival mode, I was not able to focus, organize, or process information the way other kids my age were able to. In contrast, my father always sat down with my brother to help him with his homework. No one extended the same courtesy to me. It seemed as if everything came easily to my brother. He excelled in various areas and received everything he wanted. My brother was also taught about work ethic, money management, and saving at a young age. He would often accompany my father to work at the golf course and earn a small allowance, learning valuable life skills in the process. I, on the other hand, never received that kind of guidance. My parents enrolled me in numerous extracurricular activities, but I never saw any of them through to completion. In contrast, my brother was consistently committed to the activities he had started and was encouraged to see them to completion throughout his childhood.

Despite the expectation that one should finish what one started, no one ever held me to that standard. I felt lost and aimless, lacking the direction and support that my brother received. I can recall how, during winters, my brother and I would walk to a nearby farmer's field and go tobogganing on a hill. He would dig tunnels in the snow and persuade me to go inside them.

One day, the tunnel collapsed while I was inside, and I remember my brother just standing there, laughing, offering no help as I struggled to free myself. To this day, I'm not sure how I managed to escape that situation.

On another occasion, we went for a walk on the weekends when we weren't in school, exploring our backyard. It was springtime, and we came across a small creek. As I walked on the ice, it cracked, and I fell in, my legs submerged in the freezing water. My brother abandoned me, walking away and leaving me to fend for myself. When I finally made it home, my parents scolded me for walking on the creek, while my brother faced no repercussions. It seemed like I was always the one getting into trouble, even for events that were beyond my control. In my entire childhood, I don't remember ever witnessing my parents fighting or having any altercations. Let alone any form of affection towards one another, maintaining a peculiar distance from one another. In their minds, they had done everything right: they were high school sweethearts who dated through high school, got married, built careers, had children, and stayed together, living out their version of "happily ever after." They believed this was the proper way to live, but I have always been one to forge my own path, exploring possibilities beyond their prescribed ideals.

My parents were emotionally unavailable in many ways, even during critical stages of my life. As I entered my teenage years and started experiencing puberty and hormonal changes, I found it difficult to discuss these issues with them. I remember once gathering the courage to ask my mom about shaving my legs, only for her to react with disgust, making me feel ashamed for even bringing up the topic. Such conversations were consistently shut down, and I never dared to bring them up again. In grade 12, I tried to discuss going on birth control with my mom, but she was appalled by the idea, considering me far too young for that. It was always off-limits. I recall a day in sixth grade when I was getting ready for my Tae Kwon Do class, wearing my white uniform.

My mom abruptly sent me to my room, and I soon discovered that I had gotten my period for the first time. She tossed a pad at me, telling me I wasn't going to Tae Kwon Do that day, and that was the extent of the conversation. No one ever took the time to sit down with me and discuss the birds and the bees or the changes my body was experiencing. I was left to navigate these critical stages of my life on my own, feeling isolated and unsupported. Upon reflecting on my upbringing in Haley Station, I've come to understand that while our family may have appeared perfect on the outside, the reality was far from it. Through the challenges and emotional hardships, I faced, I learned the importance of embracing my authentic self and the power of vulnerability. As I continue to grow and heal from my past experiences, I hope that by sharing my story, others may find solace in knowing that they are not alone in their struggles and that it is possible to rise above difficult circumstances to find strength, resilience, and ultimately, a sense of self-worth.

Chapter 2: The Abuse

I was the apple of my mother's eye from the moment I entered this world. As a little girl, I was the embodiment of sweetness and love. My mother often reminisces about the days when I was her precious, innocent child. But as the years passed, a transformation occurred, leaving her bewildered and questioning the fate that had befallen her daughter. She claimed that as I grew up, I became a complete bitch, the biggest bitch she had ever met.

My mother has shared with me time and time again the story of how, during her pregnancy, the doctors predicted that I would be born with spina bifida, a condition that could have left me permanently disabled. Against all odds, I was born perfectly healthy, and my mother felt blessed. However, she couldn't help but wonder if raising a child with spina bifida might have been easier than dealing with the challenges that lay ahead for me.

Growing up, I was constantly tormented by my brother. His cruel words and relentless insults about my appearance and intelligence were like a never-ending barrage. As a child, I was defenseless against his verbal abuse, and over time, his hateful words became ingrained in my psyche.

I began to see myself through the warped lens of his cruelty, and self-love became an elusive dream. For most of my life, when I looked in the mirror, I saw what my brother called me.

My attempts to seek help or share my feelings with others were repeatedly rejected and dismissed. Eventually, I learned to suppress my emotions, believing that vulnerability was a sign of weakness. I built a wall around my heart, locking away my capacity to love and feel compassion for others. Instead, I harbored a growing storm of anger, bitterness, and resentment, ready to erupt.

Unbeknownst to me, I had become a ticking time bomb, a deadly robot operating on autopilot. My true self was buried deep beneath the layers of pain and anger, waiting for the day when I would finally break free from the shackles of my past and learn to love the person staring back at me in the mirror. Little did I know that my journey of self-discovery and healing was just around the corner.

As I grew up, I struggled to find stability and love. I felt like a walking time bomb, unsure what would trigger my emotions. Fearful of revealing my true self, I sought validation from others, desperately clinging to anyone who showed me a glimmer of attention.

Holidays and special occasions were never a source of genuine happiness for me. I believed the material gifts I received were never enough, and I yearned for more, thinking they would fill the void within me. It took me years to realize that the emptiness could only be filled by learning to love and accept myself.

My relationship with my father was strained and superficial. I longed for the day when he would sit down with me, discuss life, and express his pride in me. Instead, he remained silent and distant, leaving me starved for the love and guidance a father should provide. My brother's relentless bullying took a significant toll on my life. His constant torment made me feel powerless, and I was afraid to defy him. The fear of consequences loomed over me like a dark cloud, making it impossible to stand up against his cruelty. He forced me into uncomfortable situations, leaving me feeling violated and helpless.

To this day, I am unsure of the full extent of the harm he inflicted, as my mind has likely buried some of the most painful memories to protect me.

Sex never held any sacred or passionate meaning for me. I often found myself emotionally detached and used my body as a weapon to achieve what I wanted. My brother's callous behavior extended beyond our home, affecting my relationships with his friends and those at my high school.

His malicious actions made me hypervigilant and constantly on guard, never truly feeling safe or at ease. I vividly recall a night when one of my brother's hockey friends sneaked into my room, crawling on his hands and knees to touch me. This memory, like many others, remains etched in my mind, fueling my need to always look over my shoulder.

In another instance, my brother humiliated me during my high school orientation by forcing me to sit at the front of the bus while he and his friends threw their lunch at me. He continued to taunt me throughout the day, and I couldn't understand why none of his friends stood up for me.

Those same friends who knew my connection to my brother pretended not to know me at school. I couldn't help but wonder what lies my brother had told them to manipulate them into ignoring me. Was he trying to protect himself from the consequences of his actions? My fear of frogs, often dismissed as irrational, can be traced back to childhood trauma. My brother and cousin would fill buckets with frogs, dumping them over my head and forcing me to put them in my mouth. To this day, the mere sight of a frog sends me into a state of panic, a reminder of the painful past I am determined to overcome.

Frogs were not the only reminder of the trauma I endured. My brother would torment me daily, telling me I was adopted and making me feel worthless before the day began. Once, he convinced me to climb over a fence and face a bull he claimed was put away. I narrowly escaped the danger, only for him to mock me years later for listening to him.

Growing up, I struggled with friendships. I was codependent and possessive, only able to handle one friend at a time. If they were absent, I felt lost and unable to function. This behavior stemmed from my deeply ingrained feelings of abandonment.

Throughout my life, I had four best friends, none of whom I am in contact with today. I would become jealous and feel rejected when they interacted with others, not realizing that my past was shaping my relationships.

My first best friend and I were inseparable from kindergarten to grade three. One night, during a sleepover at her house, her older brother came into the room and violated me.

This terrible incident left a deep scar on my soul, but sadly, it wouldn't be the last time I faced such abuse. In high school, I was at another friend's sister's house for a sleepover. I woke up on the couch to find a man kneeling beside me, attempting to take advantage of me. Looking at his face, I realized it was the same man who had hurt me years ago at my friend's sleepover.

The horrifying coincidence left me reeling like I was cursed to suffer endlessly. My past seemed to follow me like a shadow, a constant reminder of the pain and trauma I had endured. It felt like no matter where I went or what I did. I was haunted by the ghosts of my childhood, always waiting for the next blow to strike.

Despite the darkness that enveloped my life, I knew I couldn't let these experiences define me. I had to find a way to break free from the chains of my past and heal the wounds inflicted upon me. The road to recovery would be long and arduous, but I was determined to reclaim my life and rediscover the person I was meant to be before the pain and suffering had taken their toll.

During those difficult years, I felt I had nowhere to escape the pain. At school, I was often singled out by teachers who seemed to take pleasure in embarrassing me. They would ask me questions they knew I couldn't answer, making me feel even more isolated and humiliated. I still can't comprehend why any teacher deliberately makes a child feel uncomfortable and exposed.

A teacher seemed to have it out for me in grades six and seven from the beginning. I vividly recall the first day of school when he smashed my pencil case with a baseball bat simply because it had a picture of the Backstreet Boys. He would yell at me constantly, accusing me of having an attitude problem, and put me out in the hallway almost every day. This relentless torment continued for two years, and no one ever spoke up for me. At home, I felt just as unsafe and unhappy. I hated being there, but I also dreaded going to school. I had no sanctuary, no safe space to escape from the abuse I endured. I would spend hours in my room, listening to the Backstreet Boys and fantasizing about a better life. At school, I was envious of the other girls who seemed to have everything I lacked: attention from boys, nice clothes, good grades, and popularity. They excelled in sports and had a bright future ahead of them. My self-esteem was shattered, and I struggled to find any sense of belonging or purpose.

When I was nineteen and in college, I had an unsettling encounter at a bar with a friend. A man approached me, trying to flirt and pick me up. I immediately recognized him as the teacher who tormented me during middle school. Staring at him in disgust, I confronted him, asking if he knew who I was. The audacity of his actions still makes me uneasy to this day.

I looked at him, said nothing, rolled my eyes, and walked away. That was the last time I ever saw him. I remember my brother buying me my first cigarette pack in grade eight. He took a friend and me to a high school talent show, and I can remember every detail of that moment. That's when I started smoking, a habit that lasted for twenty years.

These experiences made me realize how many other children might be going through similar struggles without anyone knowing or speaking up for them. It's heartbreaking to think that others suffer in silence, without a voice or support to help them navigate their pain.

As a little girl, I loved dancing and singing in front of my family and anyone who would watch. I would learn all the moves from Backstreet Boys' music videos and teach them to my friends at school. We even started a little group called the Backstreet Sisters. I got a few girls together, and I would teach them choreography at recess. My school would host assemblies so we could show the school our dances. However, I remember being told at home that I wasn't good at dancing, was an embarrassment, and should stop. This made me associate dancing with negativity and shame. Eventually, I stopped dancing, believing I wasn't a good dancer.

Everyone around me was emotionally unavailable, and no one could help me resolve my issues or reassure me. To this day, I only dance with my children, and now I understand why I've never been comfortable dancing around others. I've never felt comfortable being myself or doing what I love for most of my childhood. I can remember feeling small, unloved, and unheard. I didn't know how to love or receive love, and although my parents may have said they loved me, their actions didn't match their words.

My dad used to drop my brother and me off at the ski hill on Saturday mornings to snowboard. I didn't know how to do any of it. My parents always set my brother up for lessons, but not me. He reassured my parents that he would teach me what he had learned after the lessons. But that never happened. I remember the first time he forced me to go up the chairlift with him to the top of the hill.

He was gone when we reached the top, and I was alone. At that age, I was left alone in the wilderness and felt like I had been thrown out. While I was up there alone, I knew it was either sink or swim, and I did swim. This incident led to snowboarding becoming a passion for me, and I would go off on my own whenever we went and try to pick up every boy I met on the chairlifts.

I used to seek validation by getting phone numbers and kissing others. It became an obsession for me, and I even kept a little black book to keep track of all the guys I had kissed. Whenever I felt worthless, I would look at it to boost my confidence. Although I appeared to have an unwavering confidence that others admired, it stemmed from a dark and unhealthy place of low self-esteem.

To make matters worse, my brother used to abuse me by punching me and giving me bruises physically, yet he never faced any consequences for his actions. I remember my parents gave me a Guinea pig, which I loved dearly.

One day, I came home to find it stuck in my snowboard boot, and its body had molded to the boot's lining, causing it to suffocate. The devastation I felt at that moment still stays with me today.

My life has been filled with experiences that have shaped who I am today. I have overcome many challenges and struggles, but I have also learned to appreciate the good moments and find joy in the little things. Through it all, I have realized the importance of self-love, acceptance, and healing. I am still on a journey of self-discovery, but I am hopeful for what the future holds and grateful for the strength that has brought me this far.

Chapter 3: The Boy from British Columbia

Life is a journey filled with twists and turns, and sometimes, it takes us down paths we never could have anticipated. Throughout our lives, we encounter countless people who shape us in ways big and small. Some leave lasting impressions, while others fade from memory. However, occasionally, we encounter someone who truly changes us – someone who touches our soul, leaving an indelible mark that lasts a lifetime.

To this day, I'm uncertain why my parents decided to send me away. Perhaps they believed I was too much for them to handle. I've given up on seeking closure or understanding their true motives. Unexpectedly, my parents had me pack my bags and sent me across the country to stay with my aunt and uncle for a month.

My mother's brother, the man they sent me to live with, continues to be a significant figure in my life. He's the only man who has ever treated me respectfully and made me feel truly worthy of love. A compassionate, wise, and strong police officer, his presence has allowed me to maintain faith in the goodness of law enforcement despite numerous encounters with less-than-ideal officers. His unwavering integrity and commitment to justice have made a lasting impact on my life.

As I prepared to leave, I recall my mother driving me to Ottawa airport and handing me off to an Air Canada flight attendant. Unexpectedly, she hugged me and cried uncontrollably. Her embrace was unfamiliar, as our relationship had always been strained. Even at that moment, her display of emotion felt foreign and uncomfortable. As I walked down the passenger boarding bridge with the flight attendant, tears streamed uncontrollably down my face. Concerned, she asked if I was okay. To this day, I believe she thought I was crying out of sadness for saying goodbye to my mother. In reality, my tears were of relief, as though a heavy burden had been lifted from my shoulders. I was finally safe and free, leaving my hell behind.

When I saw the Canadian Rockies, I knew I was home. I had never felt more loved and secure in my childhood than with my mother's brother and his family in British Columbia. It was an emotion I had never experienced, completely unimaginable for a child who had endured so much hurt and abuse.

The love, discipline, care, respect, and safety they provided were an indescribable blessing. I doubt they truly understand the profound impact they had on my life. During my month-long stay, we camped all over British Columbia. I vividly remember our week at Haynes Point in Osoyoos. One day, as I floated on the water, I noticed this charming guy was cruising around on a Sea-Doo, and I couldn't help but be drawn to him. With unabashed confidence, I flagged him down and asked him to take me for a ride. As we spent time together, all those dreams I'd used to escape my reality had come to life.

The emotions I experienced were beyond words. Every morning, he would greet me and my uncle at the breakfast table, and we spent every waking moment together, basking in the beauty of our connection.

We often stopped in the middle of the lake, turned to face each other, and talked for hours under the sun. Floating in the water with no judgment, we found acceptance, a bond, and a connection that felt natural and surreal. Each morning, as I emerged from the tent, he would already be sitting with my uncle at the breakfast table. We spent every waking moment together, embracing the warmth of our friendship. There was no sexual tension between us, just innocent kisses – nothing more. But, as with all good things, our time together eventually had to come to an end.

Saying goodbye to him was the hardest thing I've ever had to do. Never before had I felt so important, loved, heard, or safe. We exchanged phone numbers and addresses. As I walked away from the only person who made me feel truly loved and safe, I was overcome with emotion – it was traumatic and torturous. I hyperventilated and sobbed as he told me he loved me, but I couldn't bring myself to say it back.

No one truly understood the significance of our connection, often dismissing it as puppy love. They had no idea of the burden I'd carried my entire life.

Once I returned home, I mustered the courage to call the phone number he'd given me, but it was disconnected. I then tried writing letters to the address he'd provided, but they never came back. I couldn't help but wonder if the letters found their way to him or were lost in the void, just like the connection we once shared.

The week I spent with him had given me all the hope I needed to persevere and keep living. It was as if that one moment of happiness had shown me that there could be more, and I became determined to find it again. He became my reason to keep going, my beacon of hope. I always believed that I would see him again someday – it was only a matter of time. I remember his strong bond with his two-year-old nephew at the time, and the beauty of their relationship left a lasting impression on me. I never forgot his nephew's name, and when I had my first son, I named him after that very child. It was proof of how much that boy meant to me.

For twenty years, I never forgot about or gave up on finding him. I searched for him everywhere I went and in everything I did while keeping this quest to myself. He was the little piece of hope that kept me alive, and even though no one ever knew about it, his memory fueled me to keep going and never lose faith in the power of love and connection.

That unforgettable week with the boy from British Columbia sustained me and filled me with hope, becoming my reason to keep going. He was like a fleeting moment of pure bliss, showing me that happiness and love did exist, and I just needed to find it. I always believed I would see him again – it was only a matter of time.

In my relentless search for the boy from BC, every man I encountered became a potential reunion. It was difficult to return to a life filled with abuse and emotional neglect, but no one knew that the time I spent with the boy from BC had given me a glimmer of hope that kept me alive. However, that wasn't the only time I visited Haynes Point.

At the beginning of ninth grade, my parents completed the construction of our new house by the lake. We moved in during the summer after my first year of high school. Wanting to celebrate surviving that first year, we planned a camping trip with a group of girls. We invited about eight girls, three of whom were more acquaintances than close friends. The other girls were from another city and had parents who owned a cottage on the same road we lived on. We would see them during the summer when they came to stay at the cottage, and we became friendly acquaintances.

All of us girls went to spend the night on an island near a local campground. We reached the island by canoe, paddling with all of our belongings. As night fell, two boys from the campground approached our group, bringing beer with them. They offered drinks to all the girls, but one by one, the girls said they were tired and went to bed. Eventually, only myself and one of the boys remained, sitting by the fire outside the tents.

If I were to visit the island again today, I could pinpoint the exact tree and location where everything took place. As I sat by the fire, I began to feel that something was wrong with me. I was losing control of my body and couldn't move, even though my mind was fully aware of what was happening around me.

With all the other girls in their tents, I found myself lying on the ground, unable to move or react. I was in shock, and my body had frozen. I could feel every single motion of the boy who took advantage of my vulnerable state, but I was powerless to stop him.

I was completely motionless throughout the ordeal. I remember fixating on a paddle that was propped up against a tree nearby. I thought that if I could just move my foot enough to knock over the paddle, it would fall on a tent, waking someone up to save me. Despite my best efforts, I couldn't move. Then, suddenly, the boy was gone, and everything stopped. I remained on the ground, motionless, throughout the entire night. When I finally got up in the morning, I was a completely different person. I had never felt so alone, worthless, and uncared for. Upon returning home, I crawled into bed and didn't move. My boyfriend at the time called me, and I told him what had happened. He went to high school with my brother, so he told my brother, who informed my mom and the police.

To my dismay, absolutely no one believed me. This only reinforced my desire to keep quiet about my experiences. It seemed pointless to share the horrible things that had happened to me when, every time I did, people dismissed me and thought I was making it all up.

It has been more than twenty years since that incident, and I can still remember every detail as if it happened yesterday. Yet, no one has ever acknowledged it. I've tried to bring it up with my mom over the years, but she still insists that my memory of what I think happened is seriously flawed.

I remember lying in my bedroom, not moving, and feeling extremely depressed. I wasn't eating or functioning; I was completely broken. Then, my mom came into my room and told me to pack my bags once again as I was going back to British Columbia. At that moment, it was as if that was all I needed.

It lit a fire within me, and I quickly got up, thinking to myself that I was getting out of there. In a way, it felt like going through that traumatic experience was almost worth it if it meant leaving this place. When I returned to British Columbia for the second time, my brain automatically connected it with the idea that I was going to see the boy again. That small glimmer of hope was all I needed. Every time I got on an airplane, walking on the passenger boarding bridge held great significance for me. It had always been important, but the second time I went to British Columbia, it felt like I had left all of my hurt and trauma at the gate. As I walked across the bridge, I felt completely free. However, the moment I returned to Ontario and my home, I picked up everything right where I had left off. It was only a temporary fix, something I have struggled with my entire life.

I've always known what is wrong with me, and I know what the issue is, but no one has ever been able to show me the way or teach me how to work through my trauma, let it go, and heal myself. Despite the challenges, it was worth all the hard work to get to where I am today.

I remember arriving at Haynes Point in Osoyoos and feeling a surge of excitement. The moment we got there, I jumped out of the truck and ran around the campground like a little kid searching for a lost puppy in a movie scene. I was so sure I would see the boy again. As I ran around, I couldn't find him, so I decided to check the campground's check-in list. It had the names of all the occupants displayed for everyone to see. I was disappointed when I couldn't find his name.

Despite the disappointment, I never gave up hope. I thought to myself that maybe now wasn't the right time, but it would happen someday. I always believed it would. Just being there and recalling all the memories I had with him from the previous time I was in British Columbia was enough to give me even more hope than I already had.

So, even though more trauma and horrible experiences happened to me, I was still able to hold on to hope and believe in the possibility of a better outcome in the future. In the depths of my soul, I've come to understand the profound impact a single human connection can have on our lives. Love and hope can be found in the most unexpected moments, and these brief encounters can leave a lasting mark on our hearts, fueling our strength to face the darkest times. In a world filled with hardships and uncertainties, these connections remind us we're not alone and that there's always a flicker of light amidst the darkness.

As I reminisce on the precious moments, I shared with the boy who altered the course of my life, I am eternally grateful for the hope and love he breathed into me. Our fleeting time together kept my heart aflame, reminding me that life is full of unexpected encounters that can mend even the deepest scars and help us find the courage to keep pushing forward.

Chapter 4: Left Alone

In today's society, I find a pervasive lack of self-awareness. Many people don't possess the capacity to momentarily step back from a situation, to check in with themselves, to question - why this person is behaving as they are. From where does this behavior originate? Hurt people tend to hurt other people, yet we're so precipitous to pass judgment on others rather than realizing that everything transpires for a reason.

Sadly, our approach is often to judge, react, and brandish some kind of degrading label onto the individual in question. For me, home was not a sanctuary - it was far from safe. School offered no respite either. Everywhere I turned, I encountered isolation, forcing myself to be on constant high alert. This state of perpetual vigilance was not just tiring but soul-sapping. It rendered me hyper-sensitive to my surroundings, always braced for the next disaster, perpetually awaiting for the proverbial ball to drop.

I was ensnared in a labyrinth of my circumstances, trapped and unable to elude the abuse and the neglect. I was raised in a household devoid of the emotional and physical support that a child requires to bloom. The necessity to grapple with my internal turmoil and external feelings of insecurity was foisted onto me. Growing up in that hostile environment had a profound impact on my well-being. The repercussions were all-encompassing, infiltrating every facet of my existence. It shaped my personality, and not for the better. It was a suffocating existence, and yet, it was the only one I knew.

I found my identity intertwined with the coping mechanisms that I adopted throughout my life; mechanisms developed to shield myself. The tendency I have to self-isolate when I'm hurting or upset stems from my childhood. I was left alone, forced to navigate my turbulent emotions on my own. In times of distress, my instinctive reaction was to isolate, to shut down, to be alone. I had always been alone - that was the narrative of my entire life.

My ability to express myself has always been curtailed. I was perpetually closed off, unyielding to any thoughts of personal growth or anything beyond the storm brewing within me. And now I question - why was it an option for me to attend a different high school than my brother? I distinctly chose not to go to the same high school as him. Yet, the reasons behind this decision never really occurred to me when I was younger.

I often wondered why I was attending a different school. Why was nobody around me raising questions? Why were there no red flags for a brother and sister from the same household attending separate high schools? These thoughts consumed me.

Like much else in life, high school was where I felt out of place. I never truly fit in - not in school and not in life in general. My grades were subpar, and I refrained from participating in any activities. I was a target of bullying - both at home and at school. It was as if I was caught in an echo chamber of torment, with no respite in sight.

Reflecting upon my past, I can see it all with the clarity of hindsight. I was an angry person, steeped in sadness, drowning in depression. These emotions were not hidden away in some corner of my psyche. No, they were blatant, out there for everyone to see, displayed daily at school and at home. I recall a particular girl in high school who seemed to take great pleasure in belittling me. Her words, bristling with derision, were a constant reminder of my supposed ugliness. No minutiae about me escaped her sharp scrutiny. The criticism would fly from her mouth for all to hear - comments about my appearance, the size of my butt. Her presence became an ominous cloud that I dreaded, her path down the school hallway a storm I wished to avoid. I harbored a deep resentment for her for many years. But a recent realization washed over me - everything in my life happened for a reason.

This girl, this tormentor of mine, was likely grappling with her own demons at home. She redirected her pain and anger toward me, an unfortunate pattern that seemed to follow me throughout my life. People perceived my acceptance of ill-treatment as a sign of weakness.

High school brought more encounters, which fabricated more stories. One particular incident comes to mind - meeting a boy on a ski hill. I felt compelled to lie to him, to tell him I was eighteen. His belief in my lie brought a wave of thrill. I had always yearned to experience a house party, yet the invitation never arrived. So, I concocted a plan. I informed my parents that my girlfriend and I planned to go to the movies.

When my unsuspecting father dropped us off at the movie theater, I had arranged for this boy to pick us up. The destination was not the silver screen but the loud music and chatter of a house party. We arrived at the house party, and I was arm-in-arm with a boy who, in everyone's eyes, was the epitome of a dream boy. He was significantly older than me, likely in his early twenties. A symphony of attributes contributed to his allure - the cascading blonde hair, the ocean blue eyes, the sculpted cheekbones. The stylishness of his attire was rivaled only by the sleekness of his car. He was undeniably handsome, and with him by my side, I felt seen for the first time. The entrance to that party was an exhilarating experience.

The hushed whispers and the glances that trailed us brought me a sense of affirmation, an inexplicable sense of self-worth. Meanwhile, unbeknownst to me, my father had made his way to the movie theater only to find us absent. In those days, we were devoid of the immediate communication offered by cell phones. Oblivious to my father's discovery, we departed from the party. Our next stop was at my friend's house.

As we approached the end of my friend's driveway, a figure emerged. It was my father, his figure burning in the headlights. I recall the raw panic in his voice as he sprinted down the driveway, yelling. My friend, fearing my father's fury, exited the car in haste, and we sped away. Even my girlfriend, overwhelmed by my father's reaction, made her escape. She sought refuge in a nearby hut tucked away in a neighbor's field, waiting for the storm to pass.

With this dream boy beside me, we drove to Ottawa, seeking refuge in his mother's house. This wasn't a flight of passion or rebellion; it was an escape, a plea for understanding. Despite our precipitous departure, he was the epitome of respect and kindness. His hands never wandered, and his eyes never strayed. He was just... present. It was as if he had intuitively understood my yearning for companionship, for someone to stand by me. Throughout that night, we remained together. Nothing beyond companionship transpired between us. Meanwhile, my absence had ignited a flurry of worry. My parents, at their wits' end, had contacted the police. The law enforcement officials had reached out to my girlfriend, who, under pressure, revealed my location. The sanctuary we thought we had found was breached by the persistent call of the police. After an agonizing spell of time, I decided to emerge from our hideaway. The police assured me - no one would be in trouble.

Yet, what struck me as strange was the absence of my parents. They had not come to the police station. Instead, they sent my aunt to escort me back home.

Questions swarmed my mind - Why was my father not there? Where was my mother? Why had they dispatched my aunt to extricate me from this situation? It was all so surreal, so puzzling.

Looking back, a pang of guilt washes over me for the predicament I had put the boy in. I had dragged him into my whirlwind and tarnished him with a lie. I imagine that he carried that experience with him for the rest of his life, perhaps making him cautious to the point of seeking physical proof of age from others.

In the aftermath of that chaotic episode, I was left feeling adrift, devoid of trust, and bereft of faith in my abilities. I stood at the precipice of uncertainty; my self-belief eroded to nothingness. If one stumbles into a space of discomfort, an average individual will retreat, instinctively preserving themselves from further unease. It is not within their nature to court situations that demand validation from external sources. Unfortunately, I was never handed the blueprints of such a framework - a framework of boundaries, core values, or ethics. I was never taught to prioritize myself or to practice self-care. Instead, my teacher was neglect, and the lessons it taught me were harsh. I learned to trust only myself, knowing all too well that others around me were unworthy of that faith.

Throughout my life, I've shouldered the burden of blame, constantly held accountable for decisions that were deemed poor, decisions that emerged from a place of hurt and loneliness. These rebukes always stung, yet I swallowed them silently, choosing not to voice my discomfort, to contest their validity.

You see, it's vital to explore the root of these decisions. It's necessary to acknowledge that my upbringing and environment shaped these choices. The influences that dotted my life be it parents, peers, or community, have all played a part in the construction of my character. Regrettably, not all these influences were positive, and they etched patterns of behavior that weren't always beneficial. They led me to a place of flawed judgment, marred by self-loathing.

The imprint left by our environments and our upbringing is significant and deep-rooted. It's crucial to comprehend that our past experiences and surroundings can greatly influence our decisions, behaviors, and outlook on life. Rather than rushing to judge or assign blame for someone's transgressions, we should strive to understand the underlying cause, the root that sprouted such behaviors. Our focus should be on collective problem-solving, ensuring a healthier decision-making process in the future. Reflecting on my past, I can now comprehend the reasons behind my actions. I can observe the larger picture and understand that it's not about pointing fingers. I don't blame anyone, not anymore. I am a product of my upbringing and the environment I was raised in. However, it's equally important that each of us acknowledges the responsibility of fostering positive, supportive spaces for each other.

We must draw from within us the strength to surmount obstacles and manifest positive changes. Despite the trials and tribulations, the ultimate responsibility lies within us – to harness our resilience, to stand up against adversity, and to believe in our ability to thrive.

To be a scapegoat within a family unit can be a grueling experience. It's like traversing a precarious tightrope, always bearing the blame for matters that have little or nothing to do with you. You find yourself perpetually craving the support and recognition that seems perpetually out of reach.

What's important to remember, in the midst of this tumultuous storm, is that it isn't your fault. The onslaught has less to do with you and more to do with others projecting their own unhealed traumas and wounds onto you. A stark realization dawned upon me—I am not the architect of the way my family treated me. I did not design the blueprint for the unfair treatment I received.

As a child, I was worthy of nothing less than unconditional love and respect. Instead, I found myself in a debt I hadn't incurred, constantly settling the accounts for a family's failings and shortcomings that were not my own. As fingers pointed and accusations flew, no one paused to consider the possibility that the blame they were so freely attributing was misplaced. It was as though I was the fulcrum on which the entire family's dysfunction teetered, their missteps pivoting around me. In the theatre of our family dynamics, I was the quintessential scapegoat. Every applause that echoed in our family's halls was a hollow sound, as all their imperfections were projected onto me. I bore this weight, then and now. The only difference is my understanding of the situation and my acceptance of it.

I've come to a place of forgiveness, a space where I can identify these patterns and establish healthy, peaceful boundaries for myself. I'm aware now that this tumultuous whirlwind has nothing to do with me; rather, it is entirely about them. That's the hard truth, as clear as day.

Chapter 5: Shattered Innocence

I have always wanted to disappear, to leave my parents in an attempt to convey that I can't always be the "cause" of every problem. So many times, I imagined the day I would have all of my stuff packed and a place for refuge ready for my move-in. I would stand at the doorstep and shout at them the replies I never could before with an intensity I never thought I possessed.

I would throw my last argument and leave the house forever. To never return. But it was only possible in my dreams. At that moment, I thought there might not be any place I could be without being the odd one out. I vs. them would be the endless dilemma of my life.

Lackluster grades, an underwhelming witness to my scholastic abilities, always marked my academic journey. It wasn't as if all institutions were ready to welcome me with open arms. Yet, an irresistible yearning stirred in me to venture beyond the confines of my childhood home. It seemed like the faint glimmer of hope to flee home lay in the form of higher education. The gathered advice report from friends and family suggested that I should pursue the Police Foundations program. The allure of this suggestion lay in the fact that this college accepted average graders.

By the time the weekend passed and Monday rolled around, I laid in bed thinking about the newfound definable source to leave the bed. Yet, my mind was more of a medley of frustrating things. Together, my mother and I visited the school that had initially captured my interest, seeking both an education sanctuary and a place I could call home. During this excursion to a college campus, my mother voiced her decision, cautioning me that I would need to apply for a student loan to study at this distant college. To study afar meant grasping the elusive lifeline of a student loan, a lifeline she was unable to provide. However, a tempting offer surfaced in the darkness of her words. If I chose to stay close and enroll in the local college, she would not only bear the tuition fee burden - but, to sweeten the deal – buy me a vehicle to ease my daily commute.

What adolescent soul in their right mind would resist such an arrangement?

For a moment, soaring to new heights seemed an unattainable fantasy, but I felt the offer slip through my fingers, so I accepted the offer. Life once again presented an illusion of choice with no true alternatives. For a brief moment, the scales of decision titled, but the absence of any support system to lean on, whether mentally, emotionally, or financially, I resigned myself to attending college in a town barely twenty minutes from where I had spent my formative years.

Within the hallowed halls of academia, an unexpected friendship blossomed between me and a girl whose fragments mirrored my own broken spirit. She was a blonde beauty, captivating and radiant. Nights were her domain, where she reveled in the festivities with a natural charm. Her nights were filled with laughter and drinks, yet she effortlessly aced her exams the next day, leaving others in awe of her intelligence. The girl never had to study; she was probably one of the smartest women I've ever known. While she indulged herself in the depths of intoxication and promiscuity, I found solace in venting my emotions by pouring my heart out promiscuously. In a nutshell, we used different methods to numb the same emotional pain. There was no thought process behind these actions; I didn't know what to feel or how to feel. Promiscuity became my coping mechanism to bury my emotions beneath a layer of fleeting connections. I yearned for some form of validation to feel desired and accepted. A strained and dysfunctional relationship with parents often leaves children to face emotional and psychological ramifications. It inflicts children with a never-ending desire for intimate relations and being loved, regardless of how it is fulfilled. I found temporary respite through casual trysts, a desperate attempt to vent the pain I could no longer endure.

We would spend our nights at the bar from Thursday to Saturday, often encountering new faces from the nearby military base. We turned it into a game, keeping a tally on our refrigerator to mark each additional person we engaged with in our escapades. While she heavily indulged in drinking, I was usually there to ensure her safety and drive her home. However, one fateful night, I drank a 40-ounce bottle of strawberry vodka mixed with beer.

Predictably, I didn't make it to the bar. Instead, I ended up behind a carwash, unconscious. If it weren't for a random man who stumbled upon me and recognized me from being with my friend, I might not be alive today. He undoubtedly saved my life. I had lost control of my bodily functions and was choking on my own vomit. Without his intervention, I would have gone unnoticed and likely suffocated. The man and my friend brought me to the carwash, hosed me off, and placed me in the backseat of their car. They carried me to the bathroom in the military shacks, which served as dorm rooms for personnel. It wasn't ideal to be seen in that state, and it was clear that my excessive drinking had caused concern. I had a few more instances of drinking, and I vaguely recall three military guys who wouldn't leave me alone. Once, in the dimly lit atmosphere of a crowded bar, I found myself being persistently pursued by three military guys. Surprisingly, I somewhat enjoyed the toxic attention they showered upon me.

As the night came to a close and everyone left the bar, they convinced me to accompany them to the back parking lot. It's hard to pen down the events that followed. I would call it the combination of naiveness and neediness that made me ignore any hesitation I experienced at that very moment. Unaware of their dark intentions, I followed them to a pavilion disguised from prying eyes.

On that fateful night, my body endured an unimaginable shattering, and my soul suffered a crushing blow. They violated me and left me engulfed in torment and despair. Mentally and emotionally, I shut down and didn't know how to deal with it. My blank mind refused to provide any solution; my body was unable to cope with what was happening. I didn't know how to stop them from touching me.

I felt violated. I felt like a tramp.

How could someone make others feel like someone that they are not?

Is there a boundary to the depths of human depravity?

After the incident, I mustered the courage to report it to the police. However, they informed me that there was little they could do due to my heavily intoxicated state. The video footage showed me in a state of complete destruction, making it challenging to establish whether or not I had given consent. It seemed like a hopeless situation—three military personnel versus my word alone. Considering the undeniable evidence captured on video, it felt unjust that no charges could be pressed.

Any rational observer could see that no person in their right mind would willingly allow what transpired to happen. It clearly violated my consent, but unfortunately, the circumstances and small-town biases seemed to work against me. Perhaps my reputation for being promiscuous and unfairly associated with my friend contributed to the police's dismissive attitude.

My friend and I spent considerable time on the military base, struggling with our demons. She had experienced numerous suicide attempts, and I stood by her side through it all. She was the only person in my life with whom I could be my real self; I could share my feelings and have fun even in an emotionally wrecked state. We connected on a deep level; both damaged souls relying on self-sabotaging coping mechanisms.

It makes me ponder whether the pain we share connects people or the shared hope to overcome that pain together.... I accept that the means I pursued to suppress my emotional traumas were perilous. I understand that self-destructive coping mechanisms such as engaging oneself in promiscuity could alter the course of life. However, it didn't, fortunately, harm my reputation as much as the stigma of being attached to her tainted my own reputation. Our lives collided yet with another problem. If we were to protect ourselves, we might not have, but when it came to the character or life of another, a sense of resilience bloomed in us that was no less than that of a wonder woman. While self-protection might have led us to retreat, we discovered an extraordinary strength in safeguarding the well-being of others. In the face of adversity, we discovered an extraordinary strength akin to that of Wonder Woman herself, transcending our own personal turmoil.

It felt like I became her protector, constantly ensuring she made it home safely after nights filled with encounters with multiple men. I promised to pick her up the following morning to ensure her safe return. I would drive her and the men she left with, ensuring she avoided getting into a car with an intoxicated driver.

Yet, my efforts remained fruitless, and the last I heard about her was that she tragically spiraled into drug addiction and homelessness, still trapped on the streets of downtown Ottawa. Sadly, our backgrounds paralleled each other in many ways, but she hadn't yet found her way out of the darkness.

Our families scapegoated us, although it was never our inherent worth as human beings. They engraved the unrecoverable memories of bullying, put-downs, and abuse in our fates. It was our homes in which we were initially maltreated and pitied. In the Latin language, the word "parent" means "bringing forth."

They are held responsible for helping their children bring themselves forth into the world. But what we received in the name of parents were malignant narcissists who trashed their children with physical and emotional adversities, leaving us to experience lasting emotional instability till our last breaths.

Chapter 6: The Living Dead

We live in a world where pain and turmoil often seem to linger like shadows cast by the setting sun. My life was a story of the potential damage of the darkest storms. As if my experience of that night was not enough, I found myself captivated by a toxic man whose inner demons persistently haunted him in the form of PTSD.

My attraction toward him directly resulted from my attempt to forget the incident and move on. He was one of those military men I used to date. However, little did I know that this guy had his share of traumatic experiences while serving, especially his tours to Afghanistan. Our relationship was far from perfect, and we frequently clashed.

One day, the boiling lava of his past erupted into violence, and he attempted to lash out at me in a split second. In a desperate attempt to protect myself, I instinctively tried to close myself in the bathroom. He came after me and tried to punch me, but I managed to dodge the blow, causing him to shatter his hand against the bathroom door, which I think was made of steel or not, but I know that it wasn't made up of wood.

I stood there with my back pressed against the door, my heart pounding in absolute fear. The incident led to his arrest and eventual separation from me. This was not the first time he projected his anger and frustration on me. I remember waking up in the middle of the night strangled by him, and I absolutely couldn't breathe. I couldn't comprehend whether it was a dream or not; how could someone be this violent on a quiet and somber night? With time, I learned that he always had these horrible nightmares, breaking out night sweats. I always blamed PTSD for his violent behavior and everything that he was going through. At moments, I also found myself empathizing with him for his hidden battles, and I wanted to be that support, which was the biggest debarment of my life.

I should have ended all ties with him the day it happened for the first time. I always had been a firm believer that an abuser always remains an abuser, but I, like many other girls out there, relied on the illogical justification of abuse. I was frustrated with myself for defying my life's principles, especially those whose defiance made my life miserable.

The incident prompted authorities to intervene; he was charged, and we went our separate ways. During our time apart, being the victim of his violent menace, I made every effort to maintain emotional composure and avoid repeating the same mistake.

I managed to achieve a reasonable level of success in doing so. He, on the other hand, keeping up the persuasiveness of his personality, would always call me when he was drinking and begged me to come back. The never-ending chain of apologies, promises, and heartbreak continued.

One day, he showed up at my place uninformed. When I opened the door, I was shocked to my core to see him in front of me. Memories of the tragic night began to revisit my mind in their most authentic shape. I stood there, uncertainty gnawing at me. Neither of us seemed eager to break the tense silence that hung between us. I fidgeted, trying to find the right words, but nothing came to mind. So, I chose to wait for him to make the first move. He finally spoke, his voice laden with remorse, as he rubbed his hands down his face, struggling to find the right starting point. "I don't even know where to begin."

I retorted, "You shouldn't. No words can ease the pain you caused me."

His eyes met mine, filled with certainty and a profound sense of regret. "You have no idea how sorry I am. I can't find a single moment of relief knowing what I've done to you."

The anger within me began to build as he claimed I had no idea what he's been through. I clenched my teeth, and my fingers tightened around the edges of the door.

With emotions surging within me, I could no longer contain them. I pointed at him, the words flowing with intensity, "You have no idea! You have no idea what it's like to go through what you've put me through! To fear for your life at the hands of the man who claims to love you? To get physically sick just thinking about what he's done to you? You have no idea! None! Screw you! Screw you for doing this to me!"

The sudden torrent of emotion took me aback. Tears streamed down my face. I turned away from him, unable to bear looking at him any longer.

He tried to step inside the house, but I cut him off.

"No!" I yell, turning back to face him. "I will not allow this!"

He fell silent, and his face suddenly changed colors. It seemed he was not habitual of women showing mirrors to him. Moving nearer, he brought himself within a few inches of my face and uttered, "You'll regret this. Women like you can never maintain a healthy relationship. You should learn to forgive others..." I stood there, stunned, feeling a mix of shock and anger. How dare he lecture me about patience and forgiveness? Evidently, he wasn't genuinely sorry; he simply wanted to manipulate me.

As I struggled to pick up the pieces of my shattered heart and rebuild my life, I discovered I was pregnant with his child. The news struck me like a thunderbolt. A whirlwind of emotions shadowed my heart, threatening to engulf me. I grappled with the situation's complexities in the solitude of my turmoil.

Torn between the desire to be a mother and the weight of the trauma that had tainted our relationship, I found myself at a crossroads. I knew the path ahead was full of challenges and uncertainty, but I ought to remain determined to make the right decision for myself and my unborn child.

Conflicted and scared, I made the difficult decision to have an abortion. As the day of the procedure approached, anxiety began to engulf me, threatening to drown me in sorrow and regret. On that dreadful day, accompanied by a supportive friend, I reached the clinic, lost in pain, hoping to find solace on the other side. The cold, sterile walls of the clinic seemed to reflect the grip of my turmoil, and as I sat in the waiting room, my mind was flooded with memories, fears, and uncertainties.

When the time came for the procedure, I was guided into the operation theatre, where the dim, piercing lights seemed to predict the sentiments I would experience for the rest of my life. They performed an ultrasound during the procedure, revealing the fetus, and I could even hear its heartbeat.

The heartbeat of a tiny human, growing inside me, ignorant of the unbearable weight of his mother's difficulties. At that moment, the weight of my choice bore down on me, but I steeled myself, knowing I couldn't turn back.

Unfortunately, I didn't receive any painkillers or calming medication, so I felt every scrape and suction intensely, causing me to scream in agony. The medical staff kept telling me to *calm down*, as they couldn't continue if I didn't. Looking back, I believe the pain wasn't solely physical; it was a profound emotional and psychological release of what was happening.

After leaving the clinic, I felt like a part of my soul had been taken away, and I kept my emotions buried, never discussing the abortion or my feelings with anyone else. Despite the torment, I managed to move forward, carrying the weight of my pain locked inside, not sharing my struggles with anyone. The mask I wore to shield my vulnerability became a second skin, concealing my deepest wounds from the world.

Later on, I was again caught in a deeply complicated and tumultuous relationship with my boyfriend, who was again a military man. As we steered through the ups and downs of our connection, the clashes between us seemed to intensify, ultimately leading to a heated confrontation at a time when circumstances prevented us from being in each other's presence.

It was during this particularly heated exchange that an unexpected twist occurred. Our neighbors, presumably concerned about the commotion, took it upon themselves to call the police, escalating the situation further. When the officer arrived, much to my surprise, it turned out to be someone with whom I had shared a personal history. This situation required that any conscious and ethical man would have tried to support his former acquaintance, considering we separated on good terms.

I thought he might recognize me, but despite a clear hint of recognition on his face, he displayed no concern about the potential conflict of interest. After this, whatever I would have said wouldn't even matter because life again wanted me to realize my worthlessness compared to military personnel. This left me somewhat ashamed, questioning how my words could carry weight when pitted against his.

Life's twists and turns led me to spend significant time on the military base, where I became aware of the numerous occurrences of soldiers experiencing triggering episodes. One particular incident engraved itself deeply into my memory. We were all gathered in the kitchen when an abrupt, deafening sound pierced the air. One soldier, who had always been respectful toward me and affectionately referred to me as "pretty lady," was immediately overcome with distress. Without hesitation, he dropped to the floor, adopting an instinctive Army crawl as he sought to make his escape outside, seeking cover from an unseen threat.

I remember that incident so vividly, as if it happened yesterday. He was completely incapacitated by the emotional chaos, unable to function under the intense grip of anxiety and fear. He hit the floor and continued shouting, "Get down." For a moment, my mind wanted me to believe it was a scene straight from an action movie where the hero was trying to protect his comrades from a potential attack.

Sadly, this was not the only incident. Unfortunately, I witnessed many incidents where intense anxiety and fear debilitated soldiers. These experiences left a lasting impact on me, and I couldn't help but feel overwhelmed by the burden of it all. I struggled to comprehend the extent of the emotional turmoil they endured.

In the face of these challenges and heartaches, I pondered the importance of self-respect and its impact on how others perceive and treat us. I felt like a volleyball, tossed between soldiers, searching for an embrace of loyalty and love, yet they relentlessly hurled me away. I came to understand that healing wasn't a linear path but a journey filled with ups and downs. It wasn't a simple, straightforward route that followed predictable events but rather an intricate and often unpredictable expedition filled with twists, turns, and unexpected diversions. The healing process meandered through highs and lows, moments of progress, and moments of setbacks, challenging me at every step.

Yet, through this journey, I found strength, resilience, and a deeper understanding of myself and the complexities of healing, ultimately leading me toward growth and transformation. With each step I took, I grew stronger for myself and extended a helping hand to those around me.

Chapter 7: Not At Home

It was a turning point in my life when I decided to move out and pursue a job at the local ski hill. My nickname, *"Paris,"* stemmed from the stigmas people associated with me due to my blonde hair and playful demeanor, leading them to assume I was an airhead. To avoid any negative consequences and conform to societal expectations, I suppressed my intelligence, a behavior ingrained in me since childhood.

Unbeknownst to many, I was not just a front desk worker and snowboard instructor; I was also pursuing a degree in criminology while juggling work and school. I concealed my enrollment and dedication to work and school because I realized nobody in my social circle truly cared about me.

I finally mustered the courage to move out and get a place with some girls. I sat my parents down and told them everything. My mom immediately expressed doubt about the success of my little plan. She showed no empathy and said, *"It's not gonna work. You'll be back home in a week."*

Parents, particularly mothers, are expected to be the unwavering support system for their children, offering a helping hand when life knocks them down. When kids receive encouragement and moral uplift from their parents, they are motivated to put in their best efforts in any task to make their parents proud and happy. The belief that *"you can do it"* from a parent can be a powerful catalyst for a child's success. In my case, however, things took a different turn. Instead of being fueled by my mother's belief in me, I was determined to prove her wrong. Despite her lack of faith in my abilities, I pushed myself to the limits, juggling multiple responsibilities. This drive to show her I was capable led me to strive harder to prove her doubts were unfounded. I had always been the type to thrive on challenges, and their skepticism only motivated me further.

When I left my parent's home and started living with my girlfriends, I realized that the concept of *"having a home"* vastly differs from truly *"being at home."* Throughout my various dwellings, I never truly experienced that sense of belonging. Undeniably, each place provided me with a roof over my head, but I never got to experience the intrinsic feeling of connection to a space that I could have called *"home."*

My life soon became miserable, as it aways did. As the ski season neared its end, financial worries loomed, prompting my roommate to suggest seeking financial support from a "sugar daddy" website.

I hesitated but eventually created an account on "sugardaddyforme.com." I had encounters with older men who promised to fulfill my needs. This experience began with a meeting that felt like a job interview. I met with an older man, probably around seventy years old, but nothing substantial developed from that encounter. It struck me that he had experienced life for many years with grown-up kids way older than me, making it an odd match.

I couldn't relate to him in any way. It's quite odd to expect an emotional connection when you know the real purpose of the relationship is monetary aid. Probably deep down, I was yearning for genuine love, a friendly embrace, or at least someone would tell me that I was worthy of love and care. One such man from Cleveland worked as an advertiser. He appeared to be quite prosperous, living in a stunning house within a gorgeous neighborhood. From the outset, he seemed eager to shower me with lavish gifts and opportunities. However, my time there took an unsettling turn.

During my stay, which was initially planned for several days, everything changed in a single night. The following morning, while I was in the shower, I was taken aback to find him just staring at me. The experience was eerie and strange, filling me with a sense of impending danger.

His desires escalated rapidly, as he expressed a desire to buy me a brand-new car, even proposing marriage. It seemed as though he wanted to provide me with everything the world had to offer.

Feeling extremely uncomfortable and sensing something was amiss, I acted quickly. I pretended it was a random emergency, claiming I needed to return to Canada urgently. Within an hour, I made my escape, aware that staying any longer might expose me to even greater discomfort in his presence.

Then I came across a guy who lived in the small town of Golden, British Columbia, whose charming words and charismatic presence could captivate anyone. Little did I know that my life would intertwine with his in a way I could never have imagined.

Our paths crossed through a website, a seemingly innocent encounter in the vast virtual world. He seemed different and mysterious. In hindsight, I realize my desperation to fill an emotional void made me susceptible to his sweet promises. Against all rational judgment, I accepted his invitation to meet him in Calgary after he sent me a plane ticket from Ottawa. As I boarded the plane, a mixture of excitement and apprehension churned within me. The reckless part of my soul desired adventure to escape the mundane routine of life. But deep down, I knew I was treading a dangerous path, a path where hurt and pain often lingered.

Arriving in Calgary, the reality of my impulsive decision sank in. I was far from home, in a city where nobody knew my whereabouts except one of my close girlfriends.

As I met the man and ventured into the city's outskirts, the man's demeanor began to unnerve me. He emanated an unsettling vibe, and each minute spent in his company increased my unease. I asked for a drink to cope with my mounting anxiety, and he obliged with a bottle of whiskey.

As I sipped on the whiskey, the world blurred, and my fear dissipated. The alcohol acted as a shield, numbing me from the threatening surroundings and the reality of my precarious situation.

The man from the website who purchased the plane ticket picked me up at the Calgary airport in an RV. We drove from Calgary to Golden. On our way to his home, he pointed to a road sign, boasting about the route where he had buried women before. Fear and panic gripped my heart as I tried to maintain a façade of calmness, but inside, I was screaming for someone to rescue me. We finally reached his house on the edge of a serene lake, starkly contrasting the darkness lurking within. It was under construction, mirroring the unfinished story of my life that I had willingly stepped into. Another man, introduced as his contractor and friend, joined us. The air was heavy with tension, and I sensed something terrible was about to unfold. They escorted me to a room, which they casually referred to as a "toy room." I felt a chill crawl up my spine as they left me alone, locking the door from the outside.

Inside the room, I scanned my surroundings, trying to find any means of escape. The spooky silence outside was broken by muffled voices carrying haunting conversations from the two men. My heart pounded in my chest as I realized they were plotting unspeakable horrors against me.

My instincts screamed at me to flee, to survive. Panic set in, but I knew I had to think clearly. I called my girlfriend in a frantic plea for help. My decision not to reach out to the authorities stemmed from a deeply ingrained fear that seeking help would only worsen my situation.

For an agonizing hour, I waited, listening for the slightest hint of their movements. When the voices outside finally faded, adrenaline coursed through my veins, pushing me to take action. With trembling hands, I attempted to open the locked door, but it remained stubbornly shut.

Glimpsing my bag by the window, I made a life-altering decision. Fear and desperation fused, giving me the strength to toss my belongings outside and follow suit, jumping from the second story into the dark unknown below. My landing was far from graceful, but primal survival instincts fueled me at that moment. The adrenaline rush was both terrifying and exhilarating, a feeling I had rarely encountered in my sheltered life. My feet pounded against the ground as I sprinted toward the Greyhound bus stop. Each step brought me closer to freedom, to escape the clutches of darkness that had enveloped me.

From Calgary, I got on a flight back to Ottawa, my heart heavy with the weight of the traumatic experience. Despite the short duration of my stay in Golden, the scars it left on my soul were deep and lasting. I cut off all contact with that person, vowing never to revisit that dark chapter of my life.

I continued to encounter guys, and each time, I found myself hoping, *"Perhaps he's different from the others,"* or *"Maybe this time it will be genuine,"* or even *"It can't go wrong for the third time in a row, right?"* However, to my dismay, it ended up the same way every single time until I lost count of how many times it had happened.

Despite my traumatic experiences, I found myself trapped in this dangerous cycle, seeking temporary comfort in alcohol to cope with my decisions.

One man, Mr. Jones, had a family and met me at a hotel in Montreal. I had to consume excessive amounts of alcohol to gather the courage for each encounter. Each encounter left me feeling worthless and empty, yet I felt compelled to continue, yet the allure of money and excitement kept me trapped.

After spending a night with Mr. Jones, he gave me a substantial amount of money. Thrilled by this newfound wealth, I splurged on shopping and bills, only to discover that he had canceled the check. He threatened me, forcing me to return to him for more encounters to compensate for the money he had taken back. Amidst this phase, I also got involved with a motorcycle guy who lived nearby. He would pick me up on his bike, and I didn't give it a second thought at the time.

As I reflected on my interactions with these older men, a sense of guilt and conscience crept in. I couldn't help but wonder if I was making the right decisions in engaging with such people. It was as if I had disregarded the consequences and potential risks involved in these encounters.

Despite the immense pain and darkness in my life, I found solace in the fact that I was beginning to recognize my past mistakes. I realized that my choices had led me to this point, but I also knew it was time to break free from this destructive cycle. My journey to self-discovery and healing had just begun.

I kept finding myself in these precarious situations, seemingly piling on the trauma for myself. It's almost as if I had no regard for my well-being, giving away my body as though it held no value. This realization hits me now with a profound sense of regret.

Now, I see how I lacked the self-respect and awareness to make better choices for myself.

It's crucial for me to learn from these experiences, prioritize my safety, and develop a healthier sense of self-worth. I deserve to be treated with respect and care, not to put myself at risk or let others take advantage of me.

The harrowing encounters taught me the importance of trust, the value of intuition, and the strength that lies within when faced with unimaginable circumstances.

Sometimes, in the stillness of the night, I wonder about the paths that led me to cross with the enigmatic men. Was it a test of my resilience, a lesson in self-preservation? I may never know the answers, but I carry that experience as a reminder to be cautious, cherish every moment, and appreciate the light that drives away the shadows of the past.

Chapter 8: Falling in Love with a Sugar Daddy

I had this strange intuition that entering into this sugar daddy game might lead to some significant consequences, but never did I anticipate just how soon those consequences would come crashing into my life. It was as if the meaning of love had changed, leaving me forever altered. Usually, most girls my age fall in love with guys with that subtle combination of good looks and charm.

They seek partners of their own age, hoping for a relatable bond and the chance to experience all the wonderful things that people in their same group can joyfully share. However, my childhood trauma again surfaced and threw me off the path of conventional love standards.

It was during the chaos of emotions and vulnerabilities that I found myself falling, rather unexpectedly, in love with a sugar daddy. Yes, I fell in love with a sugar daddy. Even more astonishing was the fact that I somehow found myself embracing the little bits of love, respect, and sense of belonging that he offered me -feelings that I had longed for my whole life.

It all began on an ordinary day in the most mundane setting of a Starbucks cafe within the bustling streets of downtown Ottawa. For the longest time, I had grown accustomed to the feeling of being used and treated like some discarded piece of trash, with no one taking the time to inquire about my well-being truly. So, when this man before me asked me, "How are you?" I was taken aback, unsure of how to react to this unexpected display of kindness.

In my frustration and desperation to release the pent-up emotions, I mustered a firm "NO," ignoring whatever he might have had in mind. His response was quite surprising to me. Instead of being discouraged, he offered an alternative suggestion: "Do you want to go shopping?" It was an innocent enough proposition, and it was no secret that I loved shopping—like countless other girls. It was the common ground on which all girls could connect and start a conversation.

So, I agreed. We went to the Rideau Center in downtown Ottawa. He took me to this store that was rather bougie – quite out of my league. I had never been to a store like this before. It was as though I had stumbled into a scene from the movie "Pretty Woman."

He sat on the chair outside of the waiting room. First, he asked the store lady to pick up dresses for me, but he soon decided to do it by himself. He walked through the different aisles and picked different outfits. He then requested me to try them on. I was fascinated; it was a completely new experience for me. For the first time, someone was tending to my needs, selecting dresses for me to try on, and I couldn't help but feel valued by this care and attention.

I obliged his requests and tried on each outfit he had chosen for me. To my surprise, he had purchased absolutely everything available at the store without hesitation, which left me feeling both awkward and grateful yet powerless to resist the pull of this puzzling figure. And afterward, we started walking in the mall. We walked into the Westin hallway entrance, and he told me to wait for a moment right there. Curiosity troubled me, wondering where he was headed next. I watched him take the elevator upstairs, my mind racing with possibilities. Did he have further plans for us? Upon his return, he didn't say anything to me, and I, in my submissive state of mind, followed him without a question, suppressing any doubts that tried to creep in. The next moment, we entered a room, and I was utterly captivated by the lavishness surrounding us. It was like stepping into a world I had only seen in movies before.

He was a completely different person in the room. His earlier kind demeanor seemed to vanish, replaced by a commanding presence that made my heart race with apprehension. For a moment, I felt this didn't seem safe, but I had no choice but to listen. But again, I put myself in that situation.

While getting dressed, he asked me about the bills that I had to pay. I told him about my car insurance. He then took me to the machine and handed me a substantial sum to cover my expenses. And then we went our different ways. A few days passed, he started coming over to my house. Our relationship seamlessly turned into a normal one. We started going on dates and watching movies, and he used to bring me coffee in the morning.

Though we never explicitly discussed our relationship's nature, it felt like we were turning into something significant. He treated me with a tenderness that went beyond the sugar daddy and sugar baby arrangement. However, the unspoken question of "What are we?" Or "Where is this relationship going?" Remained in the backdrop, waiting to be acknowledged.

I distinctly recall the day when everything changed when my illusion of our relationship began to shatter. As I drove his BMW, he introduced me to designer handbags, and our life together seemed almost surreal. Flying to Las Vegas in first class. I was filled with blissful ignorance, convinced that we were a real, genuine couple. Accompanying him on a business trip to Seattle, Washington, where he had affairs to attend to at the Microsoft campus, only solidified my belief that we were in this together. Visiting his successful e-commerce company office, where he held the esteemed position of founder and CEO, I felt a sense of pride and belonging as if we were partners in life and business.

My heart was so entangled in this web of affection that I couldn't see the reality that lay before me. I never questioned his actions or intentions, dismissing any nagging doubts that tried to bring me out of this fake love relationship.

However, fate has a peculiar way of revealing truths we often overlook. So, one day, I dropped him off at the airport. I thought I would take his car over to the carwash to show my devotion as a good girlfriend. As I parked the massive car, I noticed a book underneath the backseat. I picked it up and began to read. I realized that the past year had been nothing but a lie. The diary's content revealed his marriage, his three kids, and a honeymoon.

A honeymoon - that required the bond of matrimony. Questions flooded my mind. Marriage, a honeymoon—did he have a wife? My gut churned, and my world felt like it was turning upside down. Panic and confusion enveloped my heart as I tried to comprehend the implications of what I had discovered.

I couldn't wait; I called him immediately. He was away on a business trip in New York City. I told him his car was at the airport, and I returned it, leaving the keys in the gas tank. Back home that night, he showed up at my door, pleading and confessing that he was married and only wanted me as his mistress. Memories of Las Vegas flashed in my mind. One night, I was annihilated and passed out on Las Vegas Boulevard. A stranger claimed to help me wake up, but I clearly remember him invading my private space. But thankfully, a security guard intervened, rescuing me from the situation.

I'll forever be grateful for his kindness and respect. I vaguely remember him throwing me over his shoulder. And he carried me through numerous casinos. And I was vomiting. He took me to the door of my room. I was staying at the

Venetian. And he took me into the bathroom. He turned on the shower, and he literally threw me in the shower. And he left.

That's the last time I ever saw that man. And still, to this day, I'm so grateful for him. I have no idea who he was, but I have absolutely nothing but the utmost respect for that man. The world needs more respectable people like that.

But amidst all the heartache and trauma, there was one constant source of joy—a golden retriever named Bella. I would always talk about marriage, but Jay cleverly diverted the subject with the promise of buying me a dog if I promised to leave the subject of marriage forever. Bella became my rock for fourteen years, supporting me through thick and thin.

Jay had moved in with me after his return from New York. He seemed genuinely loving, bringing me Starbucks coffee every morning and occasionally sneaking into bed early with ulterior motives. However, it all felt so real back then. Later, when we were living together in Ottawa, I discovered I was pregnant, but he insisted on me getting an abortion.

I clarified that if it happened again, I would have the baby even if I had to raise him on my own. Reluctantly, he drove me to the appointment and left me there. I felt alone and scared. Afterward, we never discussed it again.

He took me out to a restaurant with his friends and colleagues, where one of his childhood friends bullied me, calling me names in front of everyone and making me feel like a piece of trash. No one defended me, and I felt alone and scared.

He knew I was Jay's mistress. His friends and subordinates knew his wife and children, but they never cared to tell me about them -not even a hint to protect me from a fake and manipulative relationship. Or perhaps they thought I knew I was the other woman. But in reality, I had absolutely no idea that he was married and had children.

Later, Jay wanted us to move to our own place on the Quebec side, so we got a furnished condo.

He frequently left me to be with his wife and children while telling me he was on business trips. I studied criminology and worked at PetSmart with my golden retriever, which Jay had bought for me.

I usually took her to work, but I left her home that day. I had lost my house key. I clearly told Jay not to lock the door when he left.

Jay locked her inside the home with air-conditioning off and closed the windows. When I got home to discover the locked door, I knew I couldn't leave Bella in the top-floor Condo when it was scorching hot outside. I knew where Jay was, but something deep within me screamed, "I'm not supposed to be there. But something is holding me back. It's like, my subconscious knows something." I kept calling him, but he didn't answer my calls and messages. So, I decided, "I'm just gonna get the key and leave." Despite knowing something was wrong, I went to confront the truth and went to Jay's house to get the key. I saw his wife's car there and caught him with her and their kids.

They seemed like a perfect family. I left without causing a scene, but the pain was overwhelming.

I moved out the same day, and later on, when I was pregnant with my oldest son, we were in Seattle for his supposed business trip, but I spent most of the time alone in the hotel room, trying to be supportive while keeping my emotions to myself.

During that day, I spent most of my time alone, as he was busy with work at Microsoft. In the evening, he would pick me up, and we would go out for dinner before he dropped me off at the hotel and went back to work, returning late at night.

One day, while at our house, my computer crashed, and I asked him if I could use his computer as mine was having issues. I had no intention to spy on him, but we were in a relationship; we were a couple, so I had every right to see his pictures.

When I opened his photos, to my shock and devastation, I found explicit pictures of him with another woman engaging in intimate acts. These pictures were taken at a hotel in Seattle during the same time we had visited the city together.

The pain and heartbreak I felt was unbearable. I decided to move out and get my place while dealing with the emotional turmoil, and I discovered I was pregnant. He kept coming and going, promising to move back in, but I suspected he was living with someone else, which was true. The last time we saw each other, I lay beside him, our baby kicked, and I excitedly told him it was his son. He didn't seem to care and left without a word, and that was the absolute final time I ever saw that man.

Chapter 9: Motherhood

Despite having an indifferent and neglectful mother, I always believed that the most important thing a woman can do is create and raise a family. Though I never really thought about starting a family, deep down, I knew whenever it happens, I wanted it to be an ideal pregnancy, surrounded by a loving family and a supportive boyfriend at least - if not a husband.

Expecting a baby is meant to be a moment filled with joy, excitement, and anticipation. But at that moment, it felt like my world was shattered. Everything I hoped for – love, support, and financial stability – seemed like a distant fantasy. I never expected to be pregnant with someone who doesn't care about me or our baby. Sharing my news, I was met with unexpected disappointment and shame. I faced external pressure and judgments from the people who were supposed to love me.

I was already underconfident and devastated because of all the unfortunate events of the past that had tainted my thoughts. Family is expected to be the support system in such times of need. They should bring forth the positive aspects to pour life into lifeless family members.

When the doctor told me about the baby, my parents' faces flashed before my eyes. Children usually find comfort after telling their problems to their parents because they have faith in them that they will take care of them and seek solutions for them. But in my case, I was petrified to tell my parents. My parents were on their way to the airport for a cruise, and I asked them to stop by my office before they departed. My dad stayed in the vehicle, my mom came in, and I stepped away from work – away from everyone else. I took her outside, and I told her that I was pregnant. I still remember the anger and disappointment that appeared on her face. She completely ignored my emotional state and health risks. She immediately suggested abortion. That suggestion was like a deep cut.

It was like she didn't understand this was my child she had suggested getting rid of, even if the circumstances weren't ideal. I felt so alone. I recalled all the people I knew in my mind, but none was kind enough to share my grief.

Life took an unexpected turn, and I was left to deal with this on my own. It was overwhelming and frustrating. The uncertainty of the future scared me.

Building a home and raising a child alone without any support system was a nightmare. My mother refused to support me and forbade me from telling my father. "I'll tell him when we are on the cruise ship in the middle of the ocean to give him the time to cool down," she said. Seriously? Is that what she was afraid of – his anger? It almost felt as though I was trapped in a box. My parents had put me in a box to control me.

Despite the disappointment and heartbreak, I decided to find the strength within myself to face this situation. My baby deserved a chance at life, even if it wasn't the plan I had envisioned.

My parents were collecting all kinds of attention from the outside world. For an outsider, they seemed like the perfect parents, protecting their child at her lowest point. On the inside, I was constantly humiliated and shamed for my decisions, making me feel like I had committed an unforgivable sin. They tore me to a point where I thought I would never be able to become independent, to a point where I could handle the consequences of my decision on my own. I felt embarrassed to confess, but sometimes I thought my mother was jealous. She intentionally oppressed me by keeping me in a toxic cycle. She manipulated my shame and guilt into gaining attention from other people.

All the tragedies of my life combined were nothing compared to the pain and turmoil caused by my mother.

I didn't hear from my parents for two weeks after I had told my mother I was pregnant. And one day, my father showed up at my work. I was not ready for any more damage his words or behavior might have caused. So, I hid behind the front counter and told my boss not to tell him about me. I remained behind the counter sobbing until he left.

I gave myself a little time to process everything, and then, one day, I eventually faced my parents. No one said anything to me. It was never discussed. It was almost as if nothing had happened. We just continued to live our lives as though nothing had changed. However, not a single moment passed without me fearing for the future of my unborn child.

Since the night that Jay had left abruptly, I hadn't seen him at all. And he regularly called me and reassured me that everything was fine between us. He was just busy with his business. He told me everything I needed to hear to keep me satisfied and hopeful – just like normal couples. He basically breadcrumbed me into believing he would be there for me. It became more complex further along in my pregnancy. I ended up moving home, which I used to share with my parents for the last four months of my pregnancy. There's one thing to be physically present, and then there's another thing to be emotionally available for your loved ones. I wasn't physically alone; I was living with my parents, but they were not emotionally available for me to help me navigate through the difficult times.

I wanted my mother to reminisce about her pregnancy with me again and again, as any mother usually does. But I wasn't the fortunate one to actually experience my mother's excitement and participation.

I stayed in bed all day and all night, and all I did was eat my emotions. And by the time I'd given birth, I was close to 300 pounds. It wasn't majorly the baby's weight but rather the burden of the heartbreaking.

I never expected anyone to support me financially; it was understandable money is hard to earn, but what about moral support? It costs nothing other than a few minutes of your time and a few consoling sentences. My mother was with me at the time of the delivery. My father waited outside the room to hear my son's arrival. They were there, but I couldn't feel their presence.

When I woke up after delivering the baby, I found myself alone in the hospital room, grappling with the pain and fear that surged through my body. Tears streamed down my cheeks, and a sense of vulnerability washed over me. My parents had left. I was so vulnerable at the moment. The absence of a hand to hold made the experience all the more daunting. Every wave of pain seemed to echo the loneliness I felt inside. Vulnerable and overwhelmed, I clutched the tiny bundle in my arms, feeling the weight of responsibility sinking in. I missed the reassuring presence of family and friends at that moment, wishing they were here to share this precious moment with me.

Fear gripped my heart as I wondered if I could handle motherhood alone. But amidst the mixed emotions, a glimmer of hope emerged, knowing that my love for my child would guide me through this uncertain journey.

After delivering my baby, I was alone in the hospital room. Tears welled up in my eyes, and a sense of vulnerability washed over me. I felt the weight of loneliness and isolation, missing the comforting presence of my loved ones. Fear consumed me as I faced the daunting task of taking care of my newborn without any support. The room's silence echoed my inner turmoil, and I cried, feeling utterly overwhelmed and unsure of how to navigate this new chapter of life.

I tried my best to focus on breathing and stay calm and composed despite the overwhelming emotions. The room felt cold and sterile, and the silence around me only amplified my solitude. I longed for someone to share this moment with and reassure me that everything would be okay.

Finally, the moment arrived, and I held my precious baby, whose cries filled the room. I was overwhelmed with the joy of bringing new life into the world; I couldn't help but feel a pang of sadness. This should have been a moment of celebration with family and loved ones, but instead, it was a bittersweet reminder of the loneliness I experienced during the whole process. As I held my baby close, I instantly knew that God had given me this child as a source from whom I could seek strength and motivation to move on in life. At that moment, I made a pact with my little one to spend the rest of my life caring for and protecting him and giving everything I missed. Though the path ahead seemed uncertain, I was determined to be the best mother I could be for my child.

When we went home, my father was surprisingly hands-on with my son; he would take turns alternatingly staying up with me, feeding the baby. We had a schedule; I couldn't comprehend why he was so willing to be involved. But it definitely felt strange.

Until the day came when my mother told me my grandmother had cheated on her husband. And she ended up being pregnant with my father. My grandmother's husband treated my father as though he was his own. And my father was somehow able to relate to my son's story, even though the narrative was rather very different.

Suddenly, my heartbeat increased; I couldn't move even; it was something like an explosion within me. The relationship between my father and his mother suddenly made sense.

I knew the wounds we carried were not solely our own, but part of the legacy passed down through generations. These experiences had shaped my father's history and, unfortunately, had affected my upbringing. Yet, it was a heavy burden to carry.

As a single mother, you have to carry the world's weight. And I was overwhelmed by the responsibilities challenges that came from raising a child on my own; I made a lot of mistakes.

These mistakes resulted from my unhealed wounds, insecurities, and a lack of understanding for navigating these challenges.

I never imagined the realities of life would be revealed to me in such an excruciating way. The sense of loneliness and depression you feel due to the absence of financial stability is so real. It's a huge burden to carry, almost desperation, to have just anyone there to help. I was desperate to have it; it didn't matter. I just wanted somebody to be there to share their responsibilities with me.

It was basically a revolving door. Each time some problem emerges, you feel like you are standing on point zero – all efforts wasted.

Even though things seemed bleak at that time, I held onto hope. I hope that someday, things will turn around, and I'll find the support and love I have longed for both for myself and my baby.

Little did I know that going within and facing my deepest, darkest fears of my troublesome past would lead to self-healing, self-awareness, and a fulfilling life.

I often heard people saying, "Bounce back after the baby," but I decided to bounce forward and embrace the blessing of motherhood.

****

Chapter 10: Cuba

There are two people involved in bringing a child to life. And their roles don't end with a child's birth. Upbringing a child is a long and tiring process that requires equal effort from both the mother and the father. Mothers - overwhelmed by the labor and the newfound responsibility of a baby - are generally focused on the child's needs.

The father must help with the baby and emotionally support the mother to adapt to the new role easily. The drastic change in women's physical appearance requires constant reassurance from their partners. A small reminder, "You look lovely," or "Look at the glow!" It can make the day for a new mom.

Unfortunately, neither did my child receive his father's love nor did I have the warm embrace of my partner. After having AB, I gained so much weight I absolutely hated the feeling of being in my own skin. I was self-conscious. I felt nothing except disgust for myself.

I was unhappy in my skin, and no one could console me. No one would tell me how brave I have been throughout the process. Even the soft lies would have made me feel better. I needed reassurance that this was temporary yet so beautiful.

Without any shoulder to lean on, I decided to start running; I wanted my body back. However, I didn't contemplate how hard this would be. My knees couldn't handle the impact of the weight because I was so big. I had to wear knee braces and ran day and night, before meals and after, until I got into the best shape I've ever been.

As I achieved my dream body, the next task was to restore my mind. The failed attempt at another relationship left me with a broken heart. It was time to gather the shattered pieces of my heart and move on.

I decided to go on a vacation in Cuba to get over J Jay and revamp my life to become a better version of myself for my child. My girlfriend accompanied me on the trip. Despite my turbulent mind, the trip began smoothly, and I was having fun after a long time. I felt like the "old me" – who would do anything to have fun. Everything was fine for a while, and I was relieved.

One day, as I was waiting in the lobby, a young, intoxicated man began to stare at me. He was the kind of handsome that everyone wanted to be around.

He stayed there for a good half hour, his eyes fixed on me, making me anxious. Eventually, he got up and tumbled away. He wasn't easy to forget; his deep eyes flashed in my mind. He had this charm that was unusual for a guy of his age. I hadn't forgotten the first encounter when we met again. The very next day at the pool, I wasn't ready for that. I thought he stared at me yesterday because he was under the influence of alcohol, but today, he acted the same way. *He didn't,* or should I say, *he couldn't* take his eyes off me. It was really awkward. And he made himself very known to me and my friends. He was charismatic and charming.

He shared an incident from the first night he was at the resort. He had a party in his room, where even the flight attendant was present. During the hustle, the flight attendant stole all his cash. And I had to listen to his tragic story. I felt genuinely bad for him. He later told me that he had lost his credit card in the ocean. I couldn't do anything but feel sad for him.

As the days went by, I spent every waking moment with my girlfriend, going on all these trips around Cuba. My girlfriend and I continuously found him on the same excursions. He was always there, constantly watching me. And, if I ever crossed eyes with him, he would join us and somehow end up spending the entire day with us.

He even planned a day for the three of us to go to the spa for services. He had made it very clear that he was covering the cost and that it was a gift. Though he had already told me he had lost all the cash and credit cards, I still accepted. Perhaps infatuation does make you blind and almost naïve.

A few days into the trip, we met a group from Alberta and had all gotten to know a little bit about each other. Everyone went to the pool and enjoyed the drinks. While I was there, one of the girls mentioned that Steve, the mysterious guy, had gone on the trip with her and the rest of the group. I confronted this situation only to be denied, which perplexed me. I chose to ignore my better judgment. If I ever had any sense of judgment back then.

From the beginning, he had told me that he was there alone. His mother owned a jewelry store in Newfoundland, and he was a fourth-class power engineer for Suncor.

I believed whatever he told me. Our visit came to an end. I walked with him to the lobby to see him off. Just as we were about to leave the resort, the staff confronted him as he had a balance owed from the spa, amongst other accumulated expenditures. He hadn't paid any bills during his stay. The staff clarified that he could not leave the country until the dues were paid.

To my surprise, he turned to me with the most innocent face ever and asked if I could pay for his balance. It was about $700, but I was ready to get my credit card. Not for once did I question his intentions, and not only that. I also gave him cash to be able to leave the country.

I was a single mother already burdened with unlimited expenses; still, I followed my heart. He reassured me that he would email transfer me the money when he landed in Alberta. When he left Cuba, I had an epiphany. I instantly thought, "Woah, I just got scammed." The magic of his charm worked, and I was under his influence till he was back at his home.

The love cloud had parted, and there I was with no hope of ever seeing that man or that money again—however, the next day, when I opened up my email. There was an email from him and a screenshot of his plane ticket for Ottawa within a week, along with the money I had given him to leave Cuba.

I had just moved back to Ottawa from my parents' place to my apartment with my son and golden retriever. I was beginning a life on my own. Once again, trying to rebuild it. Steve called me and asked me to move to Alberta. I said, "*No, I'm a single mom. I'm just learning to get back on my own two feet.*" I won't move across the country with a man I just met. And I couldn't because there was no commitment between us.

There was no ulterior motive; there was no previous discussion about marriage. As soon as I said that, I remembered I was on the phone in the Walmart parking lot. And he said, "*Well, let's get married.*" I was shaken to my core. I wasn't accepting a proposal, especially from a guy who had exhibited so many red flags. I couldn't say anything, so he said, "*I'll let you go. I'll call you back. I'm gonna find someone that will marry us.*" I finally gave in to his demand for marriage. And even though I was reluctant, as a single mother, I needed a helping hand, someone with whom I could share the responsibilities. The night before we got married, he sat me down and told me he needed to tell me a few things before we got married.

He said he had done many things, including drugs and drug dealing. I'd never been exposed to this kind of environment. So, it sounded like a scene from the movie. He had lived an extremely dangerous lifestyle, smuggling drugs from the US to Canada.

But he promised to leave everything. For some reason, I believed him. I was so grateful at that moment because I had only invited the people I knew would not judge me to the wedding. I was promised a wedding dress, a ring, and a proper wedding in the future with all our family. And we would keep everything secret until then.

He had a sister - who was pregnant at that time - coming in from Brazil to be his best man. We ended up getting married in a parking lot in Ottawa, where he grew up.

I remember attempting to hold AB as I said my vows, saying you have a dad now; a sense of relief embraced me. I finally had someone to share the responsibilities, bear the weight of raising a child, and share the most precious memories of our lives.

Without hesitation, I packed up my life with no second thoughts and moved across the country, putting all my belongings from my apartment into storage. We only took the necessary things for myself, my son, and my dog.

After our wedding, while meeting his friends, I noticed what he told everyone was completely different from what he had told me. It's almost as though he had created a whole fake life story of himself. It was impossible to keep track of all his lies, especially when one was in his proximity. So, I believe no one knew anything about him that was true.

As a single mother, you have to work really hard to provide for your child. I worked incredibly hard to go through school, work a job, and purchase an SUV. This was a very proud moment for me. And the payoff vehicle was an even greater accomplishment for me.

But tension arose when my partner brought up his sacrifices for the move. I realized he wasn't committed, which left me frustrated and angry.

We were married, but the stress continued during a trip to Indonesia with my two-year-old son, leading to poor behavior and conflicts. Now that I think about it, it was the negative energy I projected and my inability to communicate effectively with my husband. I could not experience pleasant things and be grateful for things in front of me. I was unable to be in the moment. I had so much pressure on me.

Instead of understanding my feelings and properly addressing the root cause, I chose anger as a medium to vent out my negative thoughts. I would start petty fights in front of everyone. It didn't matter who we were with or who was around us. Today, those scenes remain in my head as the most embarrassing moments of my life. They could have made a really good reality show.

I remember the locals would get up and literally move away from us, but only to a point where they could still see the action. To see what was happening, to listen to what we were saying. They liked the drama but didn't want to be part of it.

A lifetime of hurt, the constant inner turmoil of demons I was fighting on a regular that no one knew about. The consequences of marrying a man I didn't know and what he was doing to me -just came roaring out of me. I appeared as a raging, fiery lunatic.

The fights continued, and anger amplified. Yet, he suggested having a baby. It was an attempt to make things better. For a moment, I was even thrilled because a piece of me was thinking, *well, maybe now I'll get the joy in the celebration I wanted with my first.* So, we impulsively decided to conceive.

Adding another child didn't solve our problems, as we both held unspoken expectations. Our communication remained toxic, and we wrongly believed that having another child would mend our relationship.

****

Chapter 11: The First Sign of Trouble

Upon returning to Fort McMurray, I discovered that I was pregnant with my second son. Excited, I immediately called my parents to share the news, only to be met with their disappointment due to their belief that marriage should come before having a child. Unbeknownst to them, I was already married. Their reaction was despondent and shook me to my core. I believed the news of the arrival of a grandchild would be something they would embrace with open arms.

As a mother, I could effortlessly sense how he was feeling from my son's tone. *How come my mother couldn't catch my happiness reflected in my voice? Or did they intentionally disregard my happiness only to satisfy their conscience by warning their daughter from having an illicit child?*

Over the years, I have realized we often place people in special positions in our hearts, but sometimes they don't truly belong there. By doing this, we create our own disappointments. Either way, the result of this emotional rollercoaster leaves the person feeling like they have been abandoned.

I learned to remove such people from my life because they don't deserve a place in it. Preferring psychological maturity, I stopped caring about other people's opinions.

Overlooking the sadness, my husband Steve and I began searching for a larger house to rent. Despite being pregnant, attending school full-time, managing the household, and taking care of AB, I handled the packing process alone. Despite knowing that my plate was packed with responsibilities, my husband, Steve, never bothered to offer a helping hand. His idea of offering a helping hand was hiring a moving company. On the day of the move, my husband, Steve, left for work in the morning and returned to find that the move had been completed.

Sometimes, I used to question the legitimacy of his work, even though he used to earn a decent salary but was absent almost on every occasion. However, he never let me touch on that topic. *I* was afraid to *ask him to help me pay* my school fees. I decided it would be easier to deal with it alone.

The situation left me with no choice but to take out a student loan to cover my tuition expenses. Additionally, Steve was adamant I rent out my spare bedroom to one of my husband's colleagues at that time.

Renting out the spare bedroom came with its own set of challenges. This arrangement required me to take care of all the renter's needs; for instance, from laundry to preparing his meals, I handled everything as he had to fly to Fort McMurray for work, and then he would fly out to wherever he lived in the world.

Steve maintained the utmost privacy about his finances, causing me to lose faith in myself as I struggled to address concerns without starting arguments. I felt a need to contribute equally to housework and keep the house spotless, but his expectations were demanding, and he would belittle me if things weren't perfect to his standards.

One morning, I was sick and couldn't get out of bed, so I skipped school. I took care of AB while in bed but lacked the energy to do anything else. When he returned, he found me still in bed and asked why the house was messy. He questioned what I had been doing all day. I was already frustrated by his uncompassionate response and callous behavior, so I replied with full force, "Isn't growing a human a full-time job?"

He snapped back, "Quit acting like you're the only pregnant woman in the world." With that, he left the room, and I didn't hear from him for two days.

A few days later, I got into a car accident. I had bought my dream car with the insurance money, with the promise that Steve would handle the rest of the payments. He convinced me to hide the truth from everyone and used my earnings for the payments he should have covered. Over time, my anger and hurt grew.

While I was six months pregnant, we argued, and he pushed me down the stairs, but luckily, I managed to protect my belly. Despite this, he dared to emphasize the importance of not missing school when the baby arrived and called his mother to help until I finished my studies in April.

I had a sudden emergency C-section and was back in class, shocking my teachers days later. Steve had gone to great lengths to create a false image that contradicted reality. I didn't know he had maintained contact with my teachers through email. Almost as though he was trying to keep tabs on me.

He maintained a false image of helping me with the baby only for social media photos. He ensured the world saw him as an ideal husband and father.

During the March holidays, we visited my parents with our two sons. It was the first evening when our family members on both sides gathered. Steve, at the time, and my brother went to get propane for the BBQ earlier that day. As time passed, I began to sense something wasn't right. They shouldn't have taken that long. Suddenly, my parents' home phone rang. I answered. On the other end was my husband, "Samantha, I need you right now. Don't say anything. Take your mom's car and drive down Astrolabe Road right now."

"Don't ask questions. Just do it," he said.

I could feel the panic in his voice. All I could think about was the well-being of my brother.

"You killed my brother, Steve. You killed my brother," was the only thought going through my mind at that moment.

When I drove to the location, I found an overturned car. Fortunately, my brother was safe. My husband tried to manipulate the situation, asking me to lie about the accident's cause. His father refused to support the lie, revealing that my husband had been drinking. My husband instructed me to gather evidence to blame the accident on me. The police were called, and my husband's mother and I were left to handle the situation.

He managed to escape all the consequences. On the contrary, I faced repercussions on my driving record because I was charged for seven years. And he walked away scot-free, and we never had a conversation about it. I, as always, took the hit and kept going.

I returned home and immediately began to file insurance claims to rectify the situation. I was profoundly wounded, betrayed, and manipulated. I couldn't look in the mirror. I had once again disappointed myself. I trusted the wrong man again, to the extent that it felt almost irreversible. I felt like I couldn't do anything but whatever he asked me to do. Whenever things went wrong, I was filled with the spirit to address them. But each time, it would inevitably escalate into a terrible argument, leaving me feeling guilty. He knew how to make me look bad. It's almost like I was conditioned to think that if I brought up any concerns or tried to communicate anything, the way people do in their relationships, it would just lead to a massive argument and physical abuse.

Christmas was around the corner. With a saddened heart and a broken body, I embarked on a journey to Newfoundland with Steve for his friend's wedding. His mother joined us. She had flown out previously to assist me with the kids while I was completing my exams before Christmas. Unequivocally, such an extensive journey is far from cheap, especially to Newfoundland with a family.

Throughout the time, I believed we were all attending the wedding after flying across the country. Otherwise, I would have left my kids with my parents in Ottawa on my way there. But again, something was bound to happen because I trusted my husband.

At the eleventh hour, he suddenly told me that the kids weren't invited due to a last-minute decision by the bride. This hurt me deeply. We traveled far across the country only to find out our kids weren't welcome.

It felt like I was being targeted. I was filled with anguish and ended up drinking heavily. At night, on George Street, I crossed paths with my husband. In my intoxicated state, I confronted the bride. I was forcefully removed from the bar for creating a scene. I admit that my subsequent actions don't justify my behavior, but I was frustrated and upset.

One of the groomsmen had picked me up, threw me over his shoulder, and carried me outside the bar. And they locked me out of the bar. The following morning, I was mortified.

I apologized to her on Facebook, but it wasn't enough. I now realize my husband knew about the kids all along and shifted the blame to the bride. It felt like he enjoyed the drama and pain caused by my reactions. It seemed like he had calculated this outcome.

While in Newfoundland, we spent an early Christmas with my husband's family, his sister's fiancé, and her kids, who were in Newfoundland at that time. We all shared the same house. The whole house was filled with lovely children and their beautiful laughs. I was lost in those innocent beings. The sight of AB playing with the kids provided an indescribable strength. Troubling thoughts seemed to matter less as I regained motivation from the little ones.

I can recall one night, while we were in Newfoundland, when AJ was sleeping in a playpen at the bottom of my bed. He woke up in the middle of the night, crying to be changed. I asked my husband to get up and take care of him. However, it quickly escalated as he ripped the covers off me and physically pushed me out of bed with his legs. It almost felt like he was kicking me.

I was half asleep, couldn't properly comprehend his action, and instantly reacted. I slapped him on the head. Shocked, I couldn't understand what happened; all I knew was that I had hit him. I later realized that the problem with constantly being gaslighted is that you second-guess everything you know to be true. You just give up and start believing others' perceptions.

His immediate reaction was yelling and screaming, which woke up the entire house. He was in absolute disbelief. He had just gotten the taste of his own medicine; he was vulnerable.

Everyone gathered at our door. At first, I was silenced. They all made me feel like it was my fault. Because, as a mother, it was my responsibility to take care of the baby.

"Why didn't you get up with the baby like you do every night? What was the big deal?" Everyone questioned, some with tongues, some with eyes.

I didn't think I was wrong for asking him to contribute; he was the father. However, his side of the story was the only one that was heard.

"I didn't get up to deal with the baby, so she slapped me on the back of the head," he said.

And still, to this day, that is what everybody believes...

Chapter 12: The Road to Rock Bottom

The narrative was set in stone, a tale where I was forever cast as the villain, the irrational wife who couldn't handle the responsibilities of motherhood. It was as if an invisible gavel had come down, sealing my guilt in the court of public opinion, a court that my husband presided over. He was the judge, the jury, and the executioner of my character. It was under these strained circumstances that we decided to make another significant change in our lives.

When we relocated to a more spacious residence, I was informed that we were now the proud homeowners. My husband confidently declared to all within earshot that the property was ours. I had been conditioned not to question anything; silence was imperative if peace was to be maintained.

My husband had a keen eye for the minutiae of my appearance, often pointing out details that I had never noticed before. For example, he would remark on the lines that he claimed smoking had left on my upper lip—lines that, upon reflection, never actually existed.

These comments made me seriously contemplate undergoing Botox treatments as a way to silence his critiques. Over time, these subtle, undermining comments eroded what little self-esteem I had remaining. It reached a point where I felt utterly depleted. One evening, as we lay in bed, I suffered a panic attack. I sensed that he was aware of my distress, and he assured me that he had something to alleviate my anxiety. He handed me a Percocet. "Here, this will help," he said. Little by little, he kept supplying me with Percocet. When I'd come home emotionally bruised after a draining day, he'd suggest, "Hey babe, pop one of these and have a drink. You'll feel like a million bucks." The Percocet tablets soon morphed into an addiction. He'd source them from the streets and always keep a stash at hand. Each morning, he'd leave three for me in the bathroom, a ritual that soon escalated to five, then ten. "Here's your supply for the day," he'd say casually as if handing me vitamins. I found myself increasingly dependent on them.

One night, we attended a Polynesian-themed event with a group of people he called his friends, a term I use very loosely. Before we left the house, he pushed two Percocets into my hand. "This will keep you going," he assured me. Though I was no stranger to mixing Percocet with alcohol, this night felt different. Fueled by the pills and far too many drinks, I found myself knocking back shots with his so-called friends, one after the other.

During the taxi ride back to our hotel, the cocktail of Percocet and booze hit me like a freight train. I lost the battle with my stomach and threw up all over the back of the cab driver's head. "What the hell?!" the driver shouted, pulling over immediately and dialing the cops. I had sunk to a level of inebriation where the world just faded to black; I passed out.

Police officers arrived and dragged me out of the cab. They laid me on the cold asphalt in the recovery position. Sirens wailed closer, and an ambulance pulled up. EMTs worked quickly, and the next thing I knew, I woke up in the harsh fluorescence of the ER. I was alive, but just barely.

Days later, my family doctor reached out, his voice tinged with concern. "We need to talk about your test results from the other night," he said. In his office, he looked me straight in the eyes. "Your vital organs are deteriorating at an alarming rate. Frankly, it's a miracle you're still here," he confessed. The room went silent. I felt like I was standing at the edge of an abyss, staring into nothingness.

After that hellish episode, tensions erupted between my husband and me. In the middle of a heated argument, he pulled out his phone. "You wanna see how bad you looked?" he sneered, flicking through photos he had taken that night. There I was, unconscious on the roadside, then later confined to a hospital bed. He flashed them in front of me like a weapon as if to say, "I own you, even at your lowest."

And he didn't just keep those photos locked away; he'd parade them in front of me again and again. Over time, he added to the collection, piling on more snapshots and videos that captured me at my weakest, most vulnerable moments. "Look at yourself," he'd taunt, showing me a new low I'd reached. And then he made it public. He blasted them to family, splashed them all over Facebook, and even had the audacity to show them to my own children. He weaponized my vulnerability, turning it into a spectacle for all to see.

The more I paid attention, the more I noticed disturbing trends in his behavior. Despite his lofty promises, he couldn't hold down a job to save his life. He'd drift from gig to gig within the oil field safety industry, always getting canned and always blaming it on "the market."

"There's just no work out there," he'd claim. It became a tired refrain. So, I clammed up and chose the path of least resistance. It was easier and more peaceful that way—or so I thought, for both me and the kids. Bills began accumulating like mountains of dread, each taller than the last. I found myself scrambling to brainstorm ways to bring in money, to meet the needs of my kids, and, hell, just to survive. All so I wouldn't have to depend on Mr. Unreliable. His constant insistence that we had to live in Fort McMurray, claiming it was the "land of opportunity," became increasingly baffling to me.

My day was a meticulously planned military operation that started at 3 a.m. One hour just to get myself looking somewhat human, and another to wrestle the kids into their day clothes. It was a marathon of bathing, feeding, dressing, and corralling them into the car—all so we could hit daycare by 5 a.m. I don't know, call it a 'mom thing,' but I couldn't bear to just yank my kids out of bed and dump them at daycare like sacks of potatoes. "Let someone else get them ready for the day. That's my job."

Then came my next ordeal: reaching the hospital floor by 6 a.m. for my backbreaking 12-hour clinical shift. Yeah, you heard that right—12 hours of hell on a stick. After that torment, the next chapter of my day was picking up the kids, feeding them, bathing them again, and tucking them into bed. And because the universe has a sense of humor, I'd then force myself to hit the books and work a side hustle. All of this was a desperate scramble to keep the ship from sinking.

He had one job: to cover daycare expenses. Should be simple, right? But nah, the payments started bouncing like a bad check, and so, as a consequence, my kids got kicked out of daycare.

To save my sinking academic ship, his mother swooped in to help with the kids. But let me tell you, explanations about those missing daycare payments were as scarce as hen's teeth. And let's get one thing straight—a safety officer in the oil fields isn't exactly counting pennies. We're talking a grand a day, easy.

So why were we always broke? His mom sensed it, too; she knew something was rotten in the state of Denmark. She got all 'CSI' on our house, flipping it upside-down in her fervor. It was like watching a detective show, but instead of a badge, she had the "Mother's Intuition" we all hear about. She was hell-bent on finding concrete proof to confirm her gut feeling.

Now, don't get me wrong—his mother and I had a relationship that was one part Hallmark movie, two parts soap opera. She had this Mama Bear instinct for her son, which I get; it's her kid, after all. She was quick to defend him and always there when the chips were down, but let's talk about the fine print.

See, the woman had a knack for stirring the pot. A real drama artist. She could be sugary one moment and all spice the next. While we had our share of warm and fuzzy moments, I later found out that she'd badmouth me whenever I turned my back. The trust was more fractured than a mirror in a funhouse.

Look, I get it now. Hurt people hurt people. Understanding why she acted the way she did doesn't mean I'm giving her a pass, but at least now, it makes some kind of twisted sense.

Steven, God bless him, didn't have a kind bone for his mother. Couldn't even stand being in the same room with her for more than a day. He had this uniform way of treating all women—like they were disposable. It's like he was reading from a script titled "How to Be a Manipulative Asshole." He played puppeteer with people's emotions, yanking their strings and cutting them loose when he got what he wanted.

Then, one fateful day, his mother—Mrs. Nancy Drew herself—did another one of her house inspections. This time, she stumbled into the garage and found something odd: a golf bag. She said out loud, "My son doesn't even golf. What the hell is this doing here?"

I hadn't even thought about that damn golf bag until she mentioned it. She unzipped the pockets—empty. But then, like she was unveiling a magician's final trick, she turned the whole thing upside down. Out tumbled these plastic bags, all ripped open at the top. More than a hundred, easy.

The moment she saw those, her eyes darkened. "Drugs," she muttered. "My son is on drugs. That's what's been eating him alive."

And what did Steven do? Denied it all, every last bit of it. As if lying would somehow make it go away.

Chapter 13: Escalation

I arrived home one day after one of many days, and I was planning on getting the kids ready for bed so I could hit the books undisturbed.

As if fate were laughing at me, I saw an eviction notice on the door. The hard truth fell on me like a ton of bricks. To add insult to injury, we had to be out before Christmas.

It was already December, and my exams were within the week. It also dawned on me that my parents were flying out for Christmas.

One thought after another flew through my head, exacerbating my panic mode. But I knew I was the only one who had to figure this out before it got worse.

The truth is that I was completely unaware of what had been occurring behind my back. It baffles me to this day what my ex-husband must have said to all those people for non-payments to go on for so long at the detriment of my own family. So, seeing the notice completely blindsided me. It clarified that my vehicle would be repossessed, my house would be taken away from me, and I had about two weeks to get out.

So, it was incumbent upon me to start finding a new home, move, take the kids to school, and care for them. Naturally, I was completely stressed out of my mind, but I didn't want to bring this to his attention. Once again, I had to pull up my big girl panties and continue moving forward as I did every other day. Steve had called me upstairs one day, and this happened not too long after the eviction notice because he discerned how stressed I was. I was inherently exhausted with everything I had on my plate. He offered me a plate of cocaine. He said, "Here, take this." He told me it would be the best thing for me, and I could get everything I needed to attend to.

"Just do one hit," he insisted. "Trust me, you'll love it. You'll be so productive."

Of course, I did it. It was just one hit, and I was absolutely hooked. I can admit to my actions.

I was running around like an Energizer Bunny, talking a mile a minute and knocking my to-do list out of the park.

To say that the whole experience was insane would be an understatement. I was able to go to school, clean the house, do everything with the kids, and still have enough energy to pack up and start moving.

Eventually, I found a house, completed the move, took my exams, studied, looked after the kids, ran my side hustle, and never slept or ate.

I was literally on, let's assume, cocaine pilot. With Steve, he constantly had to be in contact with me, and I thought it was just a part of who he was. He would call me sixty times a day on a regular day and text me hundreds of times on the same day.

I got used to it and never really protested. My parents visited us for Christmas, and then they left to return home soon after. To put it bluntly, it wasn't the greatest Christmas.

The day my parents left, I went to the store to purchase a few groceries and was at the cashier waiting to pay. My bank card was declined. It turned out that Steve had stolen my bank card and drained my account, leaving me without a penny to spare. This was the final straw! Or so I thought. I dashed home and asked him to get up, take his belongings, and get out of the house.

I wasn't doing it anymore. I couldn't handle it. I was falling apart. But this time, he actually listened, which was odd. I soon found his iPad and opened it to discover that he had been on dating sites the entire time we were together.

The photos that he had on his profile contained ones that included the two of us together, but he had edited me out. Of course, when I brought this to his attention and confronted him, he immediately denied everything and claimed he was being set up. His lousy explanation triggered me to the extreme.

The feeling in my stomach was like I had been sucker punched, and my whole world was crumbling even more than it already had.

I called one of his friends and asked him and his wife to look after the kids while I confronted him. He was already living without me.

He had moved out but still denied the dating site situation. The one thing he admitted to me was that he had a serious drug problem, which was nothing out of the ordinary. He said that he needed help.

He revealed to me a YouTube channel about Fort McMurray Steve from the site. I guess someone in town had been making little comedy episodes about his drug problem, which he was already known in town for. I was completely oblivious and naive to the truth of these videos. So, he started getting physical with me, which made me nervous. I tried to leave, but he grabbed me and pushed me. Whenever he got angry, he turned into someone else. He would become someone I would not even be able to recognize.

His anger would erupt, and it was as if his very soul had left his body. His eyes would turn, and he would cease to be human. It saddens me because my middle son brought it to my attention one day out of the blue.

It breaks my heart to realize I wasn't the only one to see this. My son, witnessing this unfold, disturbed me immensely. As soon as I saw him switch, I would end the confrontation. I tried to do so in the moment and stopped resisting him. I let him finish whatever he was doing just to ensure that he would stop and leave. Escalating would most likely be fatal for me because I knew he was capable of that act.

He could have seriously hurt me or my children. Once his anger lessened, I was calm with him and conveyed to him that I needed a few minutes to myself. I said I would go to the store and buy some cigarettes. I needed to take a breather and smoke. It took a bit of convincing, but he eventually let me leave.

I departed and rushed straight to the RCMP. I made a statement, and an officer came into the interview room and asked if my husband was privy to where I was. It turned out he had followed me to the police department in his work truck.

I never knew he had a habit of following me, stalking me, and tracking me. I didn't tell him anything about where I was going or what I was doing. So, to find out he just showed up was a complete shocker. Learning that about him made me even more concerned about my situation and safety. Fortunately, the police were present this time and escorted him. He was charged, and then conditions were put in place where he was required to give me space and stop conversing with me. He was ordered not to have anything to do with me or live with me. The police were the ones who accompanied him home and grabbed all his belongings once he was charged. Throughout this whole ordeal, the kids were already in bed, much to my relief.

After that, they all went outside, and he proceeded to take my SUV with my dog inside. Being in such a drastic situation, I couldn't help but think that there was nothing anyone could do to help me.

He had his work truck and everything he needed. He knew my dog was like my own child, which is why he was acting out of spite. He knew what would hurt me the most, so he chose to do that.

He also knew I needed a vehicle to get to school and daycare for my kids. He knew exactly what I depended on, and talking sense to him would be a waste of time.

All he could think was that he wanted to hurt me. I finally relented and said, "Whatever, I really don't care. Just give me my dog. Take the vehicle. Take whatever you want. Just give me my dog and my children and leave me alone."

Upon being confronted, I was relieved to see that he let my dog out of the car and drove off.

A man like Steve had no respect for any rules. It was his world, and everyone else was just living in it. I knew I had to get out of that world. I needed to get out of Fort McMurray and go home. It was too much at this point for me. I was losing myself. To make matters worse, Steve wouldn't allow my second son, AJ, to return home with me to Ontario. He had zero rights over AB, so AB was exempt in this scenario.

He made me an offer to recant my statement to the police, and he would allow me to move home with AJ under my care. He told me what to write and what to say. He then followed it up by demanding that I make a psychiatrist's appointment. I had no idea what his game was.

He finally explained that it would back up my statement and make it more convincing for the authorities to drop the charges.

So, I followed his orders and made the appointment. He ordered me to get my mental health textbook from nursing, get a notebook, and write down the symptoms of bipolar disorder. I wrote down verbatim everything in the textbook in my notebook that would get me a diagnosis of having a mental health illness.

During the appointment, I read verbatim directly from my notebook; all the relevant answers ranged from my daily life to my activities.

To this day, I wonder: did he not think it was strange that I could not speak from the top of my head? That I was answering him from my notebook? Eventually, he diagnosed me with bipolar disorder. You simply cannot diagnose someone with that kind of mental health illness by sitting with them for forty-five minutes. It just didn't make sense to me.

I used the diagnosis to retract my statement. The charges, however, were not dropped, but I was able to make it back to Ottawa with both my kids alone. Little did I know he had an ulterior motive with his little scheme, which he would use against me. It was like he was building his vault of conniving, cunning, and hurtful things to use against me later. It was his little safekeeping of evidence—false evidence—to throw back at me later in my life to make it absolute hell.

I asked my parents to come pick up my boys as soon as all of this was done, and I had permission to get them out.

My dad had driven across Canada to collect the boys. He picked them up and went straight back home with them. AB was the only one in school at the time, so he was transferred to another school in my hometown while AJ stayed home with my dad.

I later drove across Canada alone with my two dogs at the time. I solidified a house for myself in Ottawa after I was done with school. Once I settled with the kids, Steve, of course, wanted to try again.

His sister's wedding was coming up in Jamaica, and we had been aware of it for a really long time. He informed everyone that he had already paid for the plane tickets and reservations and was ready for us to go with him.

I, on the other hand, didn't want to go. I didn't want the drama, and I didn't want to put myself in a precarious situation.

But he wanted one more chance, and he begged me nonstop. The man was relentless. He then suggested that we go back to Cuba, where we met with the kids, and see what happens. He promised he would use this one last strip to decide whether or not we would stay together.

I felt it wasn't right and advised him to go to his sister's wedding. Going to the wedding and then on to another vacation was silly. He urged me to believe that he wanted the boys to accompany him. I wasn't comfortable with him around my kids at all. He had never cared for the kids alone before, and I wasn't going to take any risks anymore.

After that, he relayed to me that he had already called his sister and explained the situation to her. Apparently, she was okay with him not coming and us going to Cuba. I finally relented, and all four of us went to Cuba for a week.

It wasn't a good vacation in the slightest. I didn't have fun, and the boys didn't have fun either. We were all just sitting by the pool. I believe it was our second last day in Cuba, and we were already sick of the vacation. We were leaving shortly. The kids were already getting tired and bored.

I encouraged them to swim in the ocean all morning and then in the pool all afternoon.

Steve said, "I'm going to take the boys back to the room, get them showered, and get them ready for dinner. You take your time, come up whenever, and have some time to yourself."

I was sitting by the pool, and all of a sudden, I heard the most horrific scream. Any mom can recognize their child's voice when they are in distress, and I instantly recognized that it was my AB.

I had never heard him scream like that in my life. My heart raced, and I raced unbelievably fast to the room. Horrible, horrible thoughts were rushing through my head as I was running toward the direction I had heard the scream coming from.

AB was standing there. My sweetest little boy. He was so helpless, with large tears pouring from his eyes. He communicated to me that Steve had hit him. I looked at the massively swollen handprints in the middle of his back and on his bum. I charged to the bathroom and got in Steve's face, screaming epithets. I was yelling at him with every fiber of my being.

"Don't you ever fucking touch my children! You're going to touch someone? You hit me, not my children!" I screamed at him at the top of my lungs.

He punched me in the face, and I hauled off and punched him right back. He hit me with a double ear slap and ruptured both of my eardrums. I instantly collapsed to the floor, grasping my ears, which were throbbing with pain.

I'll never forget how I felt walking through the airport on the way home, holding AJ in my arms and holding AB's hand. The way everyone was staring at me. I can't even explain it. They knew I was going through something with the black eye I was carrying.

On top of everything else that was tormenting me and my children during that difficult time, once we got back, I learned that I was pregnant.

To this day, I don't know if that was his plan all along. To get me pregnant so that I would be forced to get back with him because he was the father. To use this to manipulate me into thinking I had to go back to Alberta, where we would work on trying to be a normal family again.

Needless to say, I did exactly that.

Chapter 14: Losing Myself and Everything

So once again, I packed up and moved my family back to Alberta, only this time it was in a quaint town outside of Edmonton. I was coerced to do so out of my husband's manipulation. He was there to ensure that I had etched into my head that I couldn't handle three kids being pregnant on my own. He furthered his power by relaying to me that he wouldn't support me financially if I didn't accept him back into my world.

He told me that the house was ours and we both owned it. I knew that was a bald-faced lie, but it was better to keep my mouth shut at that point.

All I could do was mock my fate and tell myself to buckle up because I knew in my heart, we were going to go for another roller coaster ride. Unsurprisingly, I was on my own throughout my pregnancy despite him being with me then. He never even bothered to accompany me to the doctor's appointment.

I wish I could have confronted him, but I was too emotionally and mentally drained by then. I had no strength to invest. I surrendered to the role of waking up early in the morning to get the boys ready for school, show up for them, and, at the same, show up for myself. I finally decided to do something for myself. I got myself another dog.

Animals always made me feel happy. My animals were the only loyalty I ever had besides my children. This time, I purchased a Great Dane. He was my savior. To this day, I believe he got me through my pregnancy. He never left my side. I named him Lieutenant Dan because every time I opened up the back door to call him "Lieutenant Dan!" it made me giggle. He was my hero. He slept with me and followed me everywhere. I would never go anywhere without him as my trusted companion.

When he grew up to be big enough, I had a bed on the floor beside me, and he used to sleep on it. Whenever I moved, he would move with me.

I was sitting in the bathtub one night, and Steve tried to get in with me. I vehemently rejected his advances, but he was persistent. He began to get agitated and raised his voice. Lieutenant Dan was sitting outside the bathtub by me on the floor. He jumped in the bathtub with me, the exact space Steve wanted to get in with me.

He glared at Steve and began growling at him. Whenever Steve would get aggressive with me, Dan would always stand up, guarding me with his presence. He was my protector.

The living environment when Steve was home for two or three days was still toxic. The cycle of abuse continued unabated.

To make matters worse, Steve rented out our spare bedroom to one of his friends, who was there more than he was. He didn't like how we functioned, which turned me into an absolute mess. I was hopeless and gracefully broken. The guy thought I was crazy. In his defense, he was probably right.

But he also thought that way due to what Steve conveyed. He was leading a smear campaign against me and still is today for all I know. He told the guy and anyone who listened that I was completely bonkers. I was not in a good headspace and had no energy to reclaim the narrative. No one knew the real truth.

This is the first time I am speaking up and speaking about my story, the truth. As far as my boys are concerned, they are haunted by their own demons. A lot of things unfolded between them and their father that I was not privy to. A few things still come up that trigger them.

AB confided in me not too long ago that he recalls Steve chasing him up the stairs with his belt, snapping it, and threatening to attack him. He was doing this to scare and intimidate him. He was always this way whenever he came home and didn't find the house according to his expectations. The children would become his scapegoats.

I couldn't help it because I was in my last trimester. He decided to hire cleaners by then. They were amazing people and came at the right time. They were always present in the house, picking up after all of us and lending me a helping hand in any way they could. I was grateful, of course. They provided their services, I believe, for about five months.

The only problem that arose was when I found out they weren't being paid. No one told me that there was an issue regarding their payment. I had no idea why the cleaners never brought this issue to my attention.

I found out about the lack of payment years later through a letter. I was disheartened to think those people were exploited, especially when they greatly helped me. It hurts when I think about all the people Steve has hurt throughout his life.

I read the letter and gave in to crying profusely. I felt sick. No one deserved to be browbeaten this way. It's beyond my understanding why someone would take advantage of good people like that. Steve had a habit of complaining about how tired he was. I guess that was due to all the plotting and scheming he conducted to exploit vulnerable people.

Once, Steve had the kids, and I stayed with him for a few days in Fox Creek while he was working. When we reached our destination, I saw he had rented an entire apartment. I was so flabbergasted that I couldn't believe my eyes. I discovered that he had an entirely different life outside of us.

Everything about him was secretive. He would never update me or keep me in the loop about anything. He would just make an announcement. He told me one time, he decided to sell his truck. Firstly, he never even told me he bought the truck. He just showed up with it without telling me anything about the sale.

Hence, I never knew how much he spent to buy it. But now that he was selling it, I had a myriad of questions to ask but remained quiet. It was pointless to ask because he'd lie or just snap at me.

Steve went to the DMV with us and told us to remain in the car so he could carry out his sale. I didn't see the man he sold it to, nor did I ask any single question among the pool of questions dominating my mind.

After selling the truck, I received a phone call from the dealership after six months. They demanded that I tell them where Steve was.

It came to my attention that Steve had forged a document stating that there was no lien on the truck to the DMV. So, when he sold the truck, he kept the money. I had no clue what he did with that money. It wasn't spent on our bills because none were ever paid. I was left in an incredible amount of debt from him. As if fate couldn't be any crueler to me, everything was in my name. The debt this man has left me in is astronomical.

The man who purchased the truck naturally had it repossessed because of the forged documents. The whole thing sounds like a bad joke, but it was really my life. He would destroy everything, and I would be left to pick up the pieces.

When my daughter was finally born, I had a C-section. I was relieved to have my Dad stay with us during her birth.

Steve had informed me that he had arrived home and demanded that I come home from the hospital. He had Percocets for me to ensure that I could get back to my usual routine and start doing all the housework I used to do before my pregnancy.

I was floored because he told me that he would take a few weeks off from work and stay home with me when I was in the hospital. Then, he would tend to me and the kids until I recovered. He was so convincing that I foolishly believed him. He was a master manipulator. I didn't even falter when I departed the hospital 24 hours after my C-section. The nurses advised against it, but then again, they couldn't keep me there against my will. Now I wish they had. I took my Dad to the airport, thinking all the while that I was finally going to have serious support from my husband this time. As soon as my father boarded the plane, Steve dropped the bomb on me that he was dropping us at home and going to work the next day.

The things I wanted to say to him were limited to my thoughts. A newborn baby in my arms and a man in charge was not ideal for starting a fight. He had this all figured out.

Subsequently, I remained alone with the newborn. I woke up every two hours to feed, change, and walk her back to sleep. As far as my husband was concerned, he couldn't be bothered. It was expected of me that I was to take responsibility.

However, I did have moral support in the form of Lieutenant Dan. He would be right by my side, following me, repeating my motions alongside me. He was always by my side, and that gave me some comfort. He would follow me down the hallway into the baby's room, lie down, and watch me while I fed, rocked, and then put her back to sleep. He would follow me back to bed.

Dan was my support system at the time. Whenever I used to get extremely exhausted, I would sometimes be in such deep slumber that I couldn't hear the baby's cries. I would always wake up to Dan's big slobbery jowls in my face. He would be staring at me, signaling that my baby required attention.

I also had to get up every morning to show up for the boys and prepare them for school.

Whereas Steve always had a reason to make his exit, especially when it came to his responsibilities. I recall when he was home and told me he would visit his cousins.

I was adamant in my opposition. I made it clear to him that he was to stay and help me out. He smirked at me and agreed. A few minutes pass, and I hear the garage door open and then close. I knew he had left. And I wasn't able to see him for a couple of days since his alleged visit.

It was getting to the point where I had no energy left in me. I was not taking care of myself. My own husband, in his own conniving way, remarked that I was overweight. The good thing was that I never had to be intimate with him due to my weight gain. I set my boundaries and drew the line in the sand that I warned him never to cross. I asserted some authority by forbidding him to touch me and to leave me alone in my space.

There were times when he would comply, but the majority of the time, he was mired in nonsensical fighting. He would get in my face and start patronizing me to try and get me to react. He was almost always successful in his attempts. He would push and push and push until I would snap and have an outburst.

You have to understand that this was his modus operandi. It was to make me look like the unstable one. This overreaction of outbursts has been part of my personality since childhood. It was always used against me as a weapon. That weapon would disarm me, and I would have to find alternative ways to heal from my eruption.

I learned later in life that people around me were aware of my weakness. They knew I had the tendency to trap myself in situations no matter what they did to me. All they had to do was get me to become triggered and react viciously.

That way, I would be the one to deal with the consequences. The notion of learning to overcome my loss of control and retain my temper was the key to ending this abhorrent cycle. Once that cycle ended, I felt powerful; it was a life-changing moment.

I began therapy once a week to better my mental health. I had to take the baby with me after I had dropped the boys to school. It was a group therapy. A women's group therapy. I've done many therapies, but none of them helped. Every single time, it was as if I was a broken record repeating myself over and over again.

Everyone just handed me a prescription as a temporary Band-Aid. Genuine help and support were never available. They'd just write down some antidepressants and Ativan and expect me to go my way.

I stopped using cocaine when I moved back to Ottawa. It wasn't something I forced myself out of; it was more of something I felt I didn't need to do anymore. But as soon as the same toxicity and violence returned to my life, I resorted to resuming my cocaine intake, numbing myself to my reality. You could call it my coping mechanism.

Back in Alberta, after I had my baby, I began taking ephedrine little by little to keep up with what was expected of me. I was consuming 108 milligrams of pills a day. That is an insane amount of ephedrine to take, if I say so myself.

I have to say it's a miracle that I live to see another day after consuming that amount. Day in and day out, I would take my cocaine and ephedrine just to keep me going and shut me down from all the ongoing emotions meant to tear me down.

I kept my stash in the laundry room on the top shelf. I always made sure to keep the door locked. At the time, I thought I was being safe. I even washed my hands after locking the door.

God must be on my side because it's nothing short of miraculous that my children were never impacted. Steve would supply me with the cocaine and provide me with numbers of the people to hook me up with. He had these people in his phone by the abbreviation of KFC. The man had KFC contacts in every town throughout the country. One day, he alerted me that he was coming home for me to try something new: High Heat.

I received a phone call from him. He was an hour away from the house. I had to get to him because his work truck was being towed at the time. He was pulled over for speeding, and I was blamed for the incident because he was transporting me cocaine. Steve had a lead foot. He never obeyed the speed limit, and it's not that he was just a bit over speeding. He went from 100 to 200 kilometers an hour, which is extremely dangerous.

His driver's license was already suspended. He would still keep getting speeding tickets left, right, and center. Of course, he never paid them as he never does for anything. My mind was exploding with questions by then.

The main reason is that he got a job working as an HSE specialist in the oil field with all these tickets and a suspended license. I knew you had to have a clean driving record to submit a driver's abstract when applying for a job. One day, I discovered copies of his driver's abstracts. Bits and pieces were cut up and glued together to create a squeaky-clean driver's abstract. I was dumbstruck.

Not because he did something wrong. That's nothing out of the ordinary. It was over how infantile the entire thing was.

Cutting up and gluing things together?

What was he in kindergarten?

It was too embarrassing to comprehend. He was acting like a child, erasing his reckless actions to escape being caught by his teacher. There is no accountability and no introspection of his behavior. I realized there was no way to get through to a man like that. One night, I tucked the kids in bed and descended the stairs. He handed me a drink of vodka. I saw that he was already intoxicated. I'll never forget what he said to me that night. He turned to me and told me confidently, "You're stuck with me for life. If you try to leave me, I will find you. I will follow you. I will watch everything you do, every step you take. I will know who you are with and where you are. There is no out. If you fight me, I will kill you. I will shoot you in the back of the head, dump gasoline over you, light you on fire, and put you out just before you die so they can't identify you. And I will wrap you up in a tarp, tie your body to a cement brick, and throw you into the Athabasca River. There's no getting out of this."

He was almost singing these words to me. He began laughing his evil laugh. He would always get like this.

He would get in the mood and give me his "I'll find you" rehearsed speech as a reminder. He would sometimes laugh at my reaction or lack thereof.

Nobody knew the actual intent behind this. Still, the detailed content he relayed scared me out of my soul. He dashed upstairs, and I took this as an opportunity to run out the back door. I collapsed in the snow with my bare feet. I buried my head in the snow and screamed. I had a severe breakdown. I couldn't do this anymore. I couldn't feel the cold. I couldn't feel anything. Everything around me felt so empty. I had nothing left in me.

I returned inside feeling totally defeated. I grabbed all my antidepressants and chugged down the entire bottle of vodka.

My body felt numb again, and I had completely lost my sense. It was the perfect escapism tactic for me. I stumbled upstairs and crawled back into bed. I hoped that I would never wake up the next day.

The next thing I knew, I woke up to find myself in the hospital the next day. I was numb and drained physically and spiritually. The overdose had a detrimental effect on me and nearly cost me my life. In a way, I was sad that I survived the ordeal. The doctors did a psych evaluation and determined that I had postpartum depression. All I needed was help at home and proper sleep. I was discharged soon after. Once I reached home, Steve was there to hand me his phone.

"Watch this," he said.

It was a video of him calling AB upstairs.

"Hey, AB. Come here, buddy. Can you wake mommy up and ask her to make pancakes?"

I saw on the video that AB had walked over to my lifeless body.

"Mommy, mommy, can you get up? Make pancakes," he said as he kept tapping my unresponsive body.

He continued tapping me, growing concerned, until he started shaking me to wake up.

I couldn't see it anymore. I turned it off.

He wasn't fazed. "Don't worry," he said. "I have many copies of this, and I'll make sure to keep it in case I need to send it out."

***

I would always park in the heated garage. It was cold in the winter; suddenly, Steve started barking at me, yelling at me to stop parking in the garage and leave the truck in the driveway. I refused because I had the baby with me, and it was too cold. But the only way to get him to calm down was to comply with his demands. I began parking in the driveway about a week or so after that episode.

I tried to start the car one morning, but it wouldn't work. I had a feeling that Steve was behind it. I stormed out and tried to find my Suburban. But he insisted it wasn't him. He convinced me when he called the neighbors and asked if they saw anything. Then he told me to call the police. I cooperated with his advice and called the police to report my car being stolen.

They made the report, and the insurance covered the rental. Some time went by. Apparently, the police had found it on some back road. By the time it was assessed, insurance had already paid off all the necessary repairs for it. It was in better condition than I had left it.

I was so happy and over the moon. I had my vehicle back. A few days passed, and I just got the baby down for a nap when I heard a knock on my door. It was a bailiff with a warrant to repossess the vehicle.

When he came with the warrant, it finally hit me like a cement wall.

How did I not know?

How did I not put two and two together?

He had planned the entire theft of the vehicle. He wanted the insurance to cover the costs, and he could get a free vehicle out of it. It all came together. But there was nothing I could do. I have been conditioned throughout my entire life to remain silent. Keep my mouth closed.

Once the bailiff left. I had a panic attack.

I became paranoid.

What else was he hiding from me?

I was in a state of perpetual fear and couldn't eat or sleep. I was a hot mess. I was crying nonstop. It was hard for me to even breathe. What made it all the worse was that I couldn't tell anyone about my problems or what I was going through.

I called one of Steve's friends, who was a neighbor. She came over to watch the kids.

I called my best friend for help. She talked me through my panic attack until I felt safe enough to drive off to the hospital. I ran into the ER, bawling and wailing. I couldn't speak correctly. I was hollering, sputtering, and just screaming at the top of my lungs.

This wasn't a normal cry. This was a cry of pain and immense sorrow. The hospital was shocked at my screams. They must have felt my pain because the triage nurse started crying, and even the administration clerk started to cry. It was as if I had released a plague of sorrow.

The other staff immediately mobilized and gave me a sedative to stop me. Because I was in for a psych evaluation, the security seized my wallet, shoes, and jacket. I was glad they did. I wanted to be taken care of. No disturbance and no distractions.

I needed sleep. I needed help. I still had a lot of responsibilities. When I finally arrived, the doctor who was tending to me informed me that he had received a phone call from my husband demanding they commit me to the psychiatry ward for an entire month. The doctor was already suspicious in his tone. He knew something was off. He looked at me and asked directly, "Is there something going on? This doesn't seem right."

The doctor began to investigate on his own, asking why Steve was speaking that way about me and why I was left home alone with the kids. His intuitive skills were remarkable. He knew straight away something wasn't right. He probably figured it out because he decided my presence was important for my kids, and my husband was spiteful.

My doctor discharged me and told me he would have security bring me my items so I could leave. He later returned and told me that Steve had sent one of his friends to pick up all my items, from my car keys to my wallet, because I was being committed.

The friend took away my vehicle as well. It was then I realized how serious he was in wanting to have his way. I had to take charge. I didn't have my wallet to get a taxi. He had planned to force me into feeling stranded. He did this because he knew I might resist and try to make my way back home. Only this time, I wasn't deterred.

I called my neighbor, who was watching the kids. She was surprised because Steve had already told her that he was on his way back from work because I was being committed and my vehicle was in the garage.

She heard my idea of the story, piled everyone in the car, and arrived to pick me up. After this, I was done. I had to leave.

I knew it would be an uphill battle for me and my children. I called my parents immediately and told them they had to come get AB and Bella ASAP.

They heard the urgency in my voice. My Dad was at my doorstep within 48 hours. He sped all the way until he had AB in his custody.

The process of giving away my son was unlike anything I had ever imagined. I had no idea when I would see him again. I knew this was bigger than me. It was one of the saddest moments of my life.

It would be later that I discovered that Steve had recorded the entire moment in his video. He wanted to constantly remind me that I had given my son away to exert his superiority over my guilt. He had concocted effective ways to get into my head.

I had gotten a place in Fort McMurray and decided to do my last bit of nursing. It was something I could do to at least support the kids.

Steve told me one day that he had called a lady to come and take the last two of my animals.

He told me if I was leaving, I was leaving with nothing.

He was raging by then. Threatening me, cursing me, I didn't dare fight back. I had to walk my Chihuahua and Lieutenant Dan outside, handed them off to a complete stranger, and walked away.

To this day, I cannot stop regretting doing that. Abandoning them.

I would wake up in the middle of the night from my panic attack. I would sob and look around in sheer desperation, hoping to see Daniel there. Steve would call me randomly to give me updates, which I know now were not honest. He was doing this to torture me. He would tell me that Dan hadn't eaten. He was depressed, and they believed he was dying of a broken heart. He finally relayed to me that Dan had died of a broken heart and said that to damage me. He kept jabbing those daggers into my heart again and again to provoke me. I packed up all the necessities for the kids and chose not to take all our belongings. A lot of those things had sentimental value, but I had no time to spare.

I was reassured that I would have access to these items and retrieve them later. Steve had already laid claim to some of them. There was enough furniture for him to furnish his own place and more.

It wouldn't be for quite a while until I found out that he had sold all of my belongings and the kid's stuff. He put a few things in storage and never paid the bills. He was true to his form to the very end.

I couldn't do anything because they weren't in my name, and he was already refusing to foot the bill. My guess is he was afraid of being exposed. He had to use everything in his arsenal to keep me in a state of fear and silence. Lord knows he had nothing left in his life. Once word got out, he would be nowhere.

Little did I know that choosing to leave him for the last and final time would only make things worse. Making the decision was the easy part. The action was the challenging one.

All I can tell you from these experiences is that healing is a long yet beautiful journey where you can look back at your past decisions, comprehend the lessons, and take accountability. Your chaotic roller coaster ride will only stop with God's grace. Once you have closure and acceptance, the emotions of shame, guilt, and fear will wash away organically. I will go as far as to say I am proud of every mistake I made today because I have learned from every one of those mistakes. By making the mistakes, I have confronted them and healed accordingly.

It has been the gateway to transforming me into the woman I am today. The mother that I am today.

I can discern the same problems in people who endured the same things I did and have so much compassion for them because they are where I once was. This empathy is what bonds us together in spirit.

Chapter 15: A Series of Unfortunate Events

To say that my nightmare was just the beginning would be an understatement, as it fails to capture the magnitude of my experiences. However, it is crucial to share every instance and every episode of my life, along with the terror I endured, so that anyone reading this can not only comprehend but also deeply empathise with everything I went through.

The episodes that unfolded may resemble scenes from a horror movie, but they were the harsh realities of my life. I found myself haunted and tormented not by a ghost but by a living being. This person left no aspect of my physical, emotional, and mental well-being unscathed.

I must acknowledge that, at some point, I reached my breaking point. Yet, it is of utmost importance that I narrate the entirety of my story to provide the necessary context for the events that unfolded. Unfortunately, the impact of these events extended far beyond myself and my children, affecting everyone I knew and loved. It felt as if a malevolent demon had unleashed itself upon me, refusing to relent or release its grip.

Allow me to shed light on the most significant incidents that shook my life and shattered my psyche during that dark period.

At that time, I had established my own place in Fort McMurray, Alberta. As I was pregnant with my daughter, I had taken a break from school since the previous year. Despite the challenging circumstances, I decided to take a refresher course in the spring to ensure my skills were safe and up to par for clinical settings. The course was comprehensive and condensed, demanding great effort from me. I was burdened with stress and had an overwhelming amount on my plate despite having my own home and attempting to maintain a cordial relationship with Steven. I kept a bed in the basement in case he wanted to spend time with the kids. However, he was always occupied with work, and although he claimed he couldn't provide child support due to his financial obligations in Fort McMurray, he never failed to supply drugs. For him, that was never an issue.

His condo was quite luxurious compared to my student accommodation, and I also had the responsibility of caring for the children. Nevertheless, I did my best to make the most out of the situation, believing it was the right course of action.

During that time, I was consuming a significant number of drugs, snorting an eight ball a day alongside ephedrine. Sleep eluded me entirely. My days were consumed by cleaning the house, school, studying and looking after the children. On my final day of the refresher course, I excelled in all my exams.

I felt an immense sense of pride and joy. Unfortunately, that same day, when I returned home, I was confronted by my ex-mother-in-law. She had discovered my hidden stash of cocaine. Little did I know, she had staged a photograph of my drug paraphernalia on top of my nursing books, adding notes to the Arsenal Vault, intending to use them as weapons against me later.

As soon as I finished my exams, Steve allowed me to fly back to my parents' home with the children, where we would stay for the next three months. In hindsight, it seemed all too convenient that he would simply permit me to leave without any fights or arguments during that period. I remember that flight vividly. When the pilot announced our arrival in Ottawa, tears of relief streamed down my face. I was finally home; I recall AJ teasing me for my emotional outpouring. He is the only one who still remembers that moment.

My mother generously bought me a vehicle so that I would have reliable transportation for myself and the children. I cherished that vehicle, fully aware of its significance to my livelihood and independence.

I couldn't help but notice a recurring pattern. My mother consistently went above and beyond to assist me without a hint of hesitation, particularly during difficult times. However, when things went well for me, she could never find happiness in my achievements.

A lingering sense of envy, jealousy, and malicious energy emanated from her. It was as if it were acceptable for me to remain beneath her, but the moment I showed any signs of rising above, it became utterly unacceptable. To be honest, I found her motivations perplexing and difficult to comprehend.

The kids and I spent a considerable amount of time at my girlfriend's place when we were home. One day, Steve called my girlfriend in a frantic state, demanding to know my whereabouts, even though I was standing right beside her. She chose not to tell him I was there; I overheard the entire conversation. Shockingly, he ended up threatening her, claiming that he would ruin her life if she didn't disclose where I was. I couldn't help but wonder what he could possibly do to harm her. We both blatantly underestimated him.

My girlfriend had just started a new job, which was a significant welcomed change in her life. It was a dream come true for her, providing her family with a stable income and benefits. Sadly, a few months later, she called me to inform me that she had been fired without any valid reason.

The only explanation given was that there was an anonymous complaint made against her. We both knew who was behind it, and I felt an overwhelming sense of guilt for the pain and hardship she had to endure for being my friend. Steve's handprints were all over this incident.

Steve's harassment extended beyond my girlfriend. He targeted everyone in my life, forcing them to distance themselves from me for their own safety.

By the end of the summer, the kids and I had to bid farewell to AB to drive across the country in our new car, back to the nightmare that awaited us. Upon arriving home in Fort McMurray, I headed to the basement to do laundry, only to find something unsettling.

The blankets on the bed were deliberately pulled back as if someone wanted to send me a message to intimidate me. It was obvious Steve had been in my house while I was away.

The winter in Fort McMurray was unbearably cold, with temperatures reaching as low as -50 degrees. Keeping my car warm was a top priority for a comfortable commute. One morning, I quickly ran out to start my car, and the moment I came back into the house, I received a text message from Steve:

Why did you just start your car?

Where are you going?

Similar incidents occurred when I skipped school for various reasons. Steve would text me:

Why are you skipping school?

Why are you sitting on your bedroom floor?

When I had left school early and was sitting on my bedroom floor, it sent shivers down my spine. How could he possibly know that I was sitting on my bedroom floor? Unless he was right there with me in that room.

Strange occurrences like this became a regular part of my life. Steve tormented me relentlessly, harassed me, and spread false accusations about me. The constant barrage of alarming messages from him left me feeling paranoid. I was always on edge, constantly looking over my shoulder. These incidents only grew more frequent with time, leaving me terrified. I couldn't sleep, fearing that he might be lurking somewhere, ready to harm me or the kids.

Whenever I left the kids with Steve, I would often go to the strip club. Surprisingly, no one ever approached me or made advances when I was there. It was conveniently close by, so I could easily walk. One night, I met a guy named Dylan, and our brief encounter turned into a situation-ship. When we got together, I was usually under the influence of alcohol and drugs, but he never mentioned it. One day I started noticing Steve would make snide comments and take jabs at the conversations I had with Dylan. Neither of us had shared any details about our personal lives or the struggles we were facing. Steve began to upset me by revealing disturbing things about what supposedly happened in my bedroom on nights when I was with Dylan. He disclosed intimate details that were deeply unsettling.

I couldn't help but question how Steve knew about these things. There was no way he could have known unless he was present during my time with Dylan. He would continuously ask me provocative questions. He revealed personal information about Dylan, such as the type of work truck he drove and his home address. These details I didn't know or care to know. Frankly, it was none of my business. Dylan started receiving warnings at work about anonymous complaints made against him. He became fearful of losing his job.

Steve continued to pester me, claiming that Dylan and I were always alone. He fabricated this narrative, claiming Dylan would take a pair of my undergarments with him as a souvenir every time we were intimate. When he was away from me, he would lay my undergarments on his bed, spray my perfume on them, and smell them.

This story somehow made its way to all of Dylan's friends and family through Facebook. He quickly connected the dots and realized who was harassing him, wasting no time in cutting ties with me. I didn't blame him for his decision. On top of that, all my undergarments mysteriously disappeared.

During that time, I was active on several dating sites. I took explicit and inappropriate pictures of myself and sent them to random men, seeking attention in all the wrong places. To my dismay, these photos ended up being circulated among all my friends and family, including Steve's mother. I was devastated. The only way anyone could have found those pictures was if they had gained access to my computer or phone.

One day, Steve dropped AJ off at my house. AL was already home with me, taking a nap. I refused to let Steve into the house when he dropped off AJ. This must have irritated him because he immediately tried to force his way in. AJ witnessed this entire ordeal. Steve shouted at AJ, urging him to run out the back door. I was furious at him for ordering our son to flee into oncoming traffic. He was completely unhinged.

AJ was too frightened to move. He was just a little boy, and Steve's constant yelling only terrified him further. In my frustration, I started yelling louder, instructing AJ to sit down and not move. All while I am frantically trying to push the front door shut, determined to keep that deranged man out.

The situation became too overwhelming for AJ, and he bolted for the back door. I let go of the door and ran after him. I grabbed him, picked him up, and brought him back inside, placing him firmly in the kitchen. Later, Steve twisted this story, making it seem like I had been harsh with AJ. He used this incident to gaslight me to the point where I questioned whether I had harmed my son. But now I know that I didn't.

Due to the layout of the house, I managed to keep AJ in the kitchen while holding the door at the same time. Eventually, Steve overpowered me and forced his way into the house. I immediately called 911, and the police were on their way. I kept screaming at Steve to leave my house. He, too, called 911 and exaggerated the situation in his favor.

Desperate to protect my son, I pleaded with the police to accompany me and conduct a thorough check to ensure both kids were safe and unharmed, and it was documented. Steve was charged with public mischief for this incident, and I was granted an emergency protective order to keep the kids safe. Thus, the battle in court began. Steve made it clear that he would file every possible motion against me to make my life a living hell unless I dropped the protective order and reconciled with him.

The next few days were consumed by him constantly driving past my home, sending me texts, bombarding me with messages from different unknown numbers. He would call me repeatedly, making outrageous demands. Despite my efforts to provide the police with evidence from the call records, they dismissed it as insufficient proof. It felt like he was haunting me, a constant presence in my life that I couldn't escape.

In my desperation, I turned to excessive drug use, consuming two eight balls of cocaine within a day. My dealer grew concerned. He contacted me, warning me to slow down. He threatened to cut off the supply if I didn't listen to him. Despite reminding me that I was a mother, he couldn't comprehend the war I was in alone. Really, no one could.

Court documents arrived, exposing my darkest and most shameful moments, including scandalous photos from my computer. I tried to defend myself, but no one believed me. They outright rejected the idea that Steve had access to my computer, phone, or anything else. Both Stephen and I were ordered by the court to undergo a 90-day hair follicle test, and to our dismay, both results came back positive for cocaine.

Overwhelmed with despair, I called my mom, sobbing uncontrollably. I didn't know what to do anymore. She wanted to know if I was truly addicted to drugs. I outright admitted it. Without hesitation, she sent my dad to be by my side immediately.

It was always my dad who came to support me, not my mother. I still haven't uncovered the underlying reason for her absence. Physically, my dad was there for me, but we never engaged in any meaningful conversations. There was always an awkward and uncomfortable silence between us.

My dad stayed with me, doing his best to shield me from Steve's presence. He couldn't understand why Steve seemed to be everywhere he went, and it was starting to unsettle him. Steve contacted me to boast about a "Urine test" that was about to be court-ordered. He took pleasure in taunting me, asking:

"Do you want to know how to beat it?"

By then, I was completely out of my mind. I was high as a kite, unable to sleep or think clearly. Of course, I wanted to know how to pass the test. Little did I know, he was setting me up. I followed his instructions to buy a detox drink from a specific store and drink it an hour before the test. Unbeknownst to me, he followed me, taking photos of my every move, including obtaining a copy of my receipt. I still have no idea how he managed to get hold of it. Nevertheless, I did pass the test.

Steve grew increasingly restless with me. Even his mother started reaching out to me. He would yell, threaten, and intimidate me, claiming that he always knew what I was up to and he would never stop pursuing me. To add to my torment, he would blackmail and shame me by sending private photos of myself from my computer. I knew he was using these tactics to instill fear in me, but I couldn't understand why.

Temporary permission was granted by the courts for my dad to take AL with him back to Ontario. My dad left, leaving me to face my personal nightmare alone. However, Steve's lawyer managed to have that temporary permission revoked. AL had to be immediately returned to Fort McMurray. Meanwhile, my dad had to fly back to Alberta with AL. I was terrified. I couldn't bear the thought of leaving my children alone with that unstable man, not even for a moment.

The Emergency Protection Order (EPO) was still in effect, and I had no idea what my next move should be. It was my turn to pick up AJ from school when my phone suddenly rang. The caller ID displayed an unknown name and number, and I automatically suspected it was Steve. Against my better judgment, I answered the call, and indeed, it was him. He made it clear that he would continue to harass me until I dropped the EPO and reconciled with him.

All I could muster was a defiant "Fuck you!" in response. He laughed maniacally, threatening, "I'll find you."

I ended the call and immediately received another one. Annoyed, I answered, not expecting anything different.

"What the fuck do you want?" I snapped.

To my surprise, it was an RCMP Officer on the other end. She asked if I was at home, which confused me. I confirmed that I was, and she informed me that she was on her way from Timberlea to arrest me. I was dumbfounded, having no clue what she was talking about. The officer explained that Steve had filed a complaint, accusing me of stealing his work phone, credit card, and more. I protested, crying uncontrollably, as I had no idea what she was referring to.

AJ witnessed the entire exchange, standing there silently. Immediately after, my phone rang again. It was Steve, laughing maniacally. He said, "All you have to do is drop the EPO, get back together with me, and all this goes away."

He instructed me to check AJ's backpack. Sobbing, I followed his orders. I found a Ziplock baggie containing a black cell phone, random credit cards, and debit cards. He then demanded that I get in the car and drive to his condo immediately. He would allow me to enter his underground parking garage. As soon as I arrived, he called the Constable, informing her all his belongings had been returned, and he no longer wished to pursue charges.

The Constable called me back shortly after that conversation. Little did she know, I was standing right in front of Steve. She informed me that he had contacted her to relay the news of the items being returned and the charges being dropped. She asked about a specific friend returning the items, but I had no idea who she was referring to. We bid each other farewell and hung up.

I had no friends left. Everyone close to me had been driven away. T was the only friend I had left from my hometown in Ontario.

One day, I was at school when Steve called, ordering me to get in my car and drive to Timberlea. At that point in my life, he would command, and I would obediently comply, asking, "How high?" The police showed no concern for my well-being. I felt utterly alone and powerless. All I could do was comply, so I got in my car and drove all the way to Thickwood. While I was driving, he called me once more. He informed me that upon reaching my destination, a red minivan would be waiting for me, and I had to get in. Steve further instructed me to leave my phone and car keys in my car once I transferred to the minivan. I complied as requested.

I entered the minivan. He was in disguise and drove us downtown Fort McMurray. We pulled into a random garage. As we stepped out, he became insistent and apologetic, demanding that I drop the EPO. He wanted everything to stop and go back to the way we once were. Exhausted and drained, I followed his instructions and dropped the EPO.

Steve was cold and calculated, using fear to manipulate me into doing whatever he wanted. One day, the kids were at daycare while I was at home when Steve requested to speak with me.

Masterfully, he found a way into my house. With the kids away, tensions escalated between us.

He brought up Dylan again, proclaiming that if he couldn't have me, no one else would. In his fits of rage, his eyes transformed as if he was possessed. He forced himself upon me despite my desperate pleas for him to stop. He violated me in my own home.

I fell silent and motionless. Silent and motionless...

It took me back to the first time this happened, lying there, staring at the ceiling with tears streaming down my face, waiting for it to be over. After he finished, he left. I couldn't call the police, as I knew it would only invite more repercussions, potentially fatal for me. No one cared. I felt utterly alone in this world. I surrendered to my vulnerability and carried the scars silently, never mentioning them again.

About a week later, he took the kids. It was daytime, and I managed to stay off the drugs long enough to get some sleep. I woke up to campus security in my home yelling at me and rushing upstairs to check on me.

I couldn't believe what was happening. They explained that they had received an anonymous call expressing concern for my safety and needed to ensure I was still alive. All I could tell them was that I had been taking a nap.

Once they were satisfied, they left. I went back to sleep, pushing the incident to the back of my mind.

Then, I was awakened by the sounds of the RCMP in my bedroom, stating that my ex had called them. I was furious. These people just couldn't grasp the situation. No one saw the bigger picture or read between the lines. It seemed like everyone was more hopeless than the last.

As I made my way outside, the police caught Steve lurking around my car. Thankfully, they arrested him and charged him with obstruction of justice, criminal harassment, breaching his conditions, public mischief, and sexual assault.

Apparently, he had called my mom at work, panicking, telling her that I was lying lifeless in bed, motionless for hours. Even though he provided specific details, my mom didn't care. Steve's modus operandi involved gathering information he could only obtain through spying on me.

Next thing I knew, there was a knock on my door, and I was served with an EPO. What struck me as strange was that I was only allowed access to AL, one of my children. How the judge didn't find that peculiar is beyond me.

Why just one child?

If I was truly an unfit mother, why was I permitted to care for one child and not the other? The reason given was that I posed a threat to the safety of the child because I possessed a cow prod. Steve had advised me randomly after I was served to check the kitchen closet's top shelf to see if the device was there.

Unbeknownst to me, he had hired someone to break into my home and plant the cow prod. Naturally, I checked the kitchen, and there it was. I immediately disposed of it. This instance made me realize that I consistently underestimated his desire to harm me.

I started dating this guy named Art from my hometown. I felt safe with him, even though he worked night shifts. AL and I were surrounded by neighbors, a stark contrast to the isolated area where I lived, where safety was a rare feeling.

One night at his place, a Facetime call came in from AJ. I was taken aback. I knew it was Steve's doing. I refused to fall for his tricks anymore and immediately contacted the RCMP to inform them of his actions. They assured me that an Officer would come to take my statement. An hour passed, and still, no one arrived. I called again. Same result. I gave up. Something felt off, but I couldn't quite pinpoint what was coming. AJ and AL were with Steve. By this time, I had consumed half a forty combined with cocaine; I felt sober. Suddenly, flashing lights pierced through my kitchen window, accompanied by a forceful pounding on my front window. I heard the shouts, "Samantha Buttle, you're under arrest! Come out now!" I opened the door, only to be faced with an aggressive officer. He arrested me and tossed me into the back of the police cruiser.

I pleaded with him to see reason and to do his job properly. But he dismissed my cries. The fact that no one would listen or care made me feel like a burden. I spent ten long hours in jail, a humbling experience, to say the least.

After those ten hours, the door finally opened, and the officer informed me that I was free to go. I asked why I hadn't been given a bail hearing. He explained that there was insufficient evidence to charge me. In my mind, I cursed at the cop, and from the expression on my face, I could tell he had read my thoughts, too.

AB called me one day, sounding incredibly sorrowful.

He said, "Hey, Mom, I know what I want for Christmas this year. I don't want any presents under the tree. All I want is my Mommy."

At that moment, I knew I would be home for Christmas with all my children, come hell or high water.

Once again, my children were being used against me. Steve was doing everything in his power, within the confines of the court, to disable me completely. He was determined to make my life unbearable. He informed me that he would grant written consent for me to leave with the kids for Christmas, but only on the condition that I reconcile with him and retract my statement regarding the sexual assault. I wrote the recantation statement, apparently his lawyer said it wasn't good enough. He had it sent back to me. I had to rewrite the statement the way he wanted it. He finally got what he wanted, and in return, I got my kids home for Christmas. The moment AB saw me with his brother and sister walk through my parent's front door was worth every hardship it took to get to him.

When I returned to Fort McMurray after Christmas, Art suddenly wanted me to move in with him, but I was naturally hesitant. Eventually, I agreed to his offer on the basis that I did feel safe with him. I was always at his place. So, it wouldn't really be any different.

Steve was predictably angry at the revelation and decided to do what he did best. He began harassing Art at work. He dug around and found one of his baby mamas. Steve and his mom interrogated this poor woman to get dirt on Art to hurt me.

Steve called me one day, urging me to hear him out. I wondered what he wanted to tell me and decided to listen. He told me to walk into Art's bathroom, the top drawer on the right side of the cabinet. He wanted me to open it and then decide for myself what I was going to do. I hung up the phone and did as I was told. Sure enough, I found a good amount of meth paraphernalia.

I was livid. I had to get away from Art and leave. It's not that I was judging him, but I couldn't risk being with someone who could cost me custody of my kids; I was already a mess. I ended things abruptly with Art.

I began selling things online that were no longer of use to me. This man named Marcus King on Facebook wanted to purchase anything I was selling. He provided me with his address, which was quite a distance from my residence. When I arrived, I found it to be an old, abandoned house. There was no one around. I was disturbed. It all felt too creepy, and I decided to turn around and leave. I never heard from Marcus King again until I was at home in Ontario for Christmas. He messaged me, saying it was Steve, and desperately wanted to talk to the kids.

I could not understand what was happening and started to freak out. Of course, he tried to gaslight me, telling me I was being crazy.

I received a phone call when I was home with the kids for Christmas. My car was being impounded. It was being impounded because Steve was caught drinking and driving at a ride program.

I was driving home one day and remembered the kids needed milk for the morning. So, I pulled into the gas station, and lo and behold, who jumped in my car? Steve.

No one knew where I was. So how did he? He keeps getting away with everything.

I randomly decided to pick up a recorder at Staples one day, coming home. I thought it could possibly help me protect myself. By the time I got back in the car, Steve was parked beside me. Somehow, he knew where I was and walked into the store to obtain a copy of my receipt to see what I had bought. It was hard to believe these things were happening, it became my normal. If the police had taken the time to do their job, none of this would have ended the way it did. No matter what I said to the police, they never took it seriously or just didn't care. It was like screaming at a wall. Nobody was hearing me. How was I supposed to get away from something like this? I was pulled into the police department by the arresting Officer when Steve was charged with sexual assault. It turned out that Steve and his mom went in and somehow convinced the Officer, with enough doubts, to interrogate me. I was scared because I didn't trust the process. It had let me down before.

The Officer was getting into my head and making me second-guess myself. He offered to do a polygraph. I was exhausted and wondered if the test would turn out in his favor and haunt me forever. I decided just to keep my mouth shut and let him do whatever he wanted with me.

One day I had a woman call me to tell me what had happened when I was in Ontario for Christmas. She asked me to meet with her so she could tell me everything. I recorded the entire conversation on my GoPro.

Her revelations were damning. Steve had hired her to break into my house while I was gone for Christmas to get a laptop. When I returned, I noticed things were stolen from my house, but I chose to remain silent. There was nothing I could do; getting anyone to hear me was a waste of energy. It came to my attention that she was a drug addict; hence, our conversation held no merit.

The police didn't care for it, which was par for the course. When I was walking out of the police station, the investigating Officer said.

"Be careful. This is a textbook domestic homicide." I kept staring at her incredulously. I just walked away. One night, Steve sent out a mass message to my friends and family on Facebook, trashing me. Thirteen people reached out to me to bring this message to my attention. I could only imagine how many others read it and chose not to engage in the drama. I did, however, report it to the RCMP just to hear their response. Freedom of speech was their defense, and there was nothing that could be done.

I had an appointment with children's services one day. Steve couldn't have known I was there. This time, I had a worker who made sure we took the precautions to be safe. The number of calls from Steve and his mom reporting me was alarming and really disturbing. When we were done with our meeting, I was about to leave the office.

Making light of the situation, I said to the social worker, "Imagine Steve is outside watching me." Both of us laughed, shrugging it off, thinking no there's no way.

Sure enough, when I walked outside, he was there, right beside my car, looking in my window. I didn't waste a second. I took his photo and managed to record a video of him running away. He got into his truck and drove off. What happened next was the least shocking part. He got off scot-free.

There were no repercussions whatsoever. He managed to manipulate his way out of it again.

I had a Police Officer call me one day to share with me what a horrible mother she thought I was. She told me that I had mental health problems and I needed to go to the hospital to get help.

Constantly on guard and looking over my shoulder, I couldn't get the feeling that I was being stalked and watched out of my head. It was outrageous.

I'll never forget the day AJ came to me and said, "Mommy, Daddy has this black magic button."

Instantly, I took the bait. I said to him, "Wow, that sounds cool. Tell me about it."

He said, "Daddy presses it, and we sit on the couch, eating popcorn and candy, and we watch Mommy."

I needed to know more. "Buddy, what do you mean you watch me?"

"We watch you all over the house, in the bathroom, sleeping everywhere. We follow you all the time, too."

It wasn't the news that disappointed me. It was that my son was being taught all of this at such a young age. It was devastating.

Steve ended up being arrested in the new year and spent a few months in jail. I can't recall.

I was alone in my bedroom, instantly taken back to Steve telling me about my alarm clock and AJ telling me Steve was watching me in my bedroom. I was so paranoid; it sounded like a ticking time bomb. Out of nowhere, I felt like it was only going to be a matter of time before it exploded. I grabbed it, rushed downstairs, and took it apart. I really thought my alarm clock was a bomb. I grabbed my kids and put them in the car, calling the police while doing so.

The police and fire departments arrived. Of course, they found it was just an alarm clock. I was so far gone that no one believed or entertained me anymore. I could only imagine what everyone who was looking at me was thinking. I had an epiphany right there. I had to leave. I had to take the kids and leave. When you are told to take your children and leave now before it's too late by people who are a part of the system implemented to protect you but know they can't help you or use it to assist, you know in your heart that the time has arrived for you to depart.

I decided to start packing my things. Since it was standard procedure, I called my dad.

He was at the doorstep, ready to help with the packing. I felt the need to try at least to go about leaving the legal way first; if all else failed, I would leave anyway while Steve was in jail. I applied for permission without Steve's consent to leave. My lawyer pointed out to me that something like this had never been done in the history of Canada before. Basically, my chances were slim to none.

However, I was granted permission to make an emergency relocation with my children without the permission of Steve. The moment I got to safety, my heart, body, mind, and soul shut down. I felt everything wash away within me. It was over.

At least, I thought it was over. I couldn't move. I had absolutely nothing left in me. I couldn't function even if I tried.

I'm not trying to justify my drug use. I feel people tend to look at individuals who have an addiction or substance abuse issue with sheer judgment instead of curiosity. They don't make enough time to understand that everyone has a unique reason behind them.

Ask yourself what kind of horrific trauma this person is trying to mask. Everyone has their own unique pain that they are trying to numb with their addiction. They don't care to find out the root cause. It's all statistics and bad news. I speak as a survivor. Someone who has managed to endure and live through an experience that others may not have survived, let alone overcome this level of decline in their mental health.

This is my primary motive for writing this book. So that anyone who has cemented hostility toward those struggling with addiction can look at them with a new lens. It's easy to judge, dismiss, and go about your business, especially when the victim in question is neither your family member nor your friend. But once the same addiction impacts a loved one, only then do you realize the reality.

My plea for anyone who thinks that drug addicts are a nuisance and bring nothing but problems is to try and be part of the solution. Change how you look at these individuals and use any means to support their rehabilitation and recovery. It is possible. I am a testament to that. I bet if you ever sat down with me today to have a conversation or passed me on the street, you would never know this was a part of my history.

You can save millions of lives just by saving one. All it requires is the ability to listen, investigate, and care. Hopefully, this sense of responsibility can collectively spread once it starts individually, and we can rescue those crying out for help.

Chapter 16: Reunited

A few months passed, and I found myself back at my parent's house, desperately seeking solace and healing from the wounds of my past. Finally free from the clutches of drugs, I longed for a fresh start.

One fateful day, as I sat at the nursing station, I logged into my Facebook account, to find the boy from British Columbia slid into my DMs. It was an unexpected surprise that would soon turn my life upside down. Against all odds, he boarded a plane and came crashing into my life like a wrecking ball, sweeping me off my feet. My heart was overcome with a mixture of disbelief, gratitude, and a pinch of 'this is way too good to be true.'

He showered me with what I believed to be love, giving me hope that this could be my happily ever after—a reprieve from the torment I had endured. But deep down, I knew I was broken and toxic, not ready to let anyone else into my shattered world. The mere thought of vulnerability terrified me.

One day, a compassionate woman from my neighborhood knocked on my door. She handed me a basket filled with words of encouragement, books, a Bible, and tools to help me embark on a healing journey. Although I couldn't bring myself to acknowledge it at the time, I stashed it away in the depths of my closet, knowing that someday I might be ready.

But as time went on, Oliver swiftly took control of my life. He demanded access to my personal accounts and sought to dominate every aspect of my existence. It all happened so rapidly, leaving me little time to process everything. When his mistreatment became unbearable, I struggled to find a way to express my emotions. In moments of frustration, alcohol became my only coping mechanism. Gradually, he imposed his religious beliefs upon me, insisting that I only listen to Christian music. The deterioration of my identity and freedom started slowly but surely. He took me back to British Columbia, hoping to recreate our childhood memories. It was at that moment, amidst the nostalgia, that he proposed. But fear of commitment and marriage consumed me, rendering me incapable of finding the right words to respond.

All I could do was weep and embrace him, though deep down, I knew I could never marry him or anyone else. We drove across Canada to my hometown with all of his belongings. His strategy was to get a house so we could move in together. He would continue flying back and forth from Fort McMurray for work.

He convinced me to sell my car, assuring me that his truck would be sufficient. His persuasive nature overwhelmed me, although perhaps I was simply naive. He wanted us to move back to Alberta, but I adamantly refused. I wanted no part in any of it. Then, he began pressuring me to have more children, incessantly pushing and pushing. The thought of bringing more children into this world, only to be left alone to raise them, filled me with an overwhelming sense of terror.

I had explicitly pleaded with my mom not to accompany him on the house-hunting adventure. I simply wasn't ready to take that step. While I was toiling away at work, my mom and he decided to take all my kids to see this exquisite house.

Naturally, everyone became excited. The children's hopes soared, but deep within me, I was torn. He persistently pushed me to find a wedding venue and a dress.

We were at my friend's one day, and he happened to glance at my phone and discovered a message from another man. I thought it was harmless, as he was just a friend who had recently reentered my life.

He lost control and caused a scene in front of everyone. I was overwhelmed with embarrassment. We left, and he went as far as to track down the man's workplace. He rode his bike there to confront him, ensuring that everyone knew I was now with him.

I endured countless toxic behaviors. He would nitpick the smallest things, sometimes resorting to tears in an attempt to manipulate me with guilt. And when that failed, he would sleep in his truck.

His immaturity was evident. He would persistently push until I apologized for something that wasn't even my fault. Then, one day before he left to return to Fort McMurray, he caused an even bigger scene than usual. I tried my best to ignore it, but then he dropped the bombshell: he was breaking up with me.

He was leaving. My world crumbled. Now, as I reflect back, I realize it was a blessing in disguise. I now understand that I was deeply triggered. His departure brought back painful memories of feeling abandoned during my childhood for the very first time. That's when we finally went our separate ways.

I rapidly spiraled downhill after he left for the airport. I pleaded with him to stay, but he remained cold and cruel. It felt as though he was reveling in the attention of me begging him. In a moment of despair, I impulsively took a dangerous amount of pills, around 500 different ones. It wasn't planned. It was an impulsive act born out of anguish and sheer desperation. I texted him, informing him of what I had done, hoping it might make him reconsider leaving. Instead, he called my mom and disclosed my suicide attempt to her.

I was in the bathroom, uncontrollably vomiting, barely able to move. My mom entered to check on me. As I lay there on the floor, feeling vulnerable and shattered, she looked at me with disgust. I will never forget the way she looked at me.

She had this twisted smirk on her face! She even put her foot on me as if she were taunting me with it, shaking me while asking what was wrong.

She mocked me.

"Trying to end your life again?" she sneered. "Should I assist you or leave you here to rot?"

Those words inflicted more damage upon me than he ever did. It was as if I couldn't possibly be more broken than I already was.

Then my dad arrived, and my mother told him she didn't know whether to take me to the hospital or not. There was no way I was going anywhere with her. I would have rather stayed there and wasted away on the bathroom floor. My dad couldn't comprehend why I refused to let my mom take me.

I kept her cruel behavior concealed, but it came at a great cost to myself. Eventually, they called the police and an ambulance. I remember being in the ambulance, hyperventilating. My mother's actions consumed my thoughts, causing me to forget about my own predicament. I simply couldn't believe what she had done. I attempted to focus and inform the paramedic about my suicide attempt, but my mother's actions kept replaying in my mind. Nothing else mattered anymore, not even Oliver.

The story I shared with the paramedic caught her off guard. Perhaps she still remembers it to this day.

Anyway, Oliver returned to my side and, out of nowhere, suggested that we move in together since things had become unbearable between him and my mom. The relationship had turned toxic and explosively volatile. While I'm uncertain about his reasons, it was primarily due to how she treated me.

We eventually found a house in Manotick, just outside of Ottawa. Oliver opened a bank account in his name and gave me a bank card, insisting that all my money should go into his account. Little did he know, I kept my own accounts. I had a feeling there was some hidden agenda behind his desire for control, both over my finances and myself.

Living together in Manotick was a bittersweet experience. On the one hand, it provided a much-needed respite from the strained atmosphere between my parents and I. However, I couldn't escape the overwhelming feeling that Oliver was exerting control over every aspect of my life, including my finances. It was as if he wanted to have complete authority over me.

Despite his insistence on depositing all my money into a bank account with his name on it, I made the decision to maintain my own secret account, as I mentioned earlier. It gave me a fragile sense of independence and security, knowing that I still had some control over my finances. I knew that revealing this to Oliver or trying to reason with him would only lead to more futile arguments and chaos.

Unfortunately, Oliver's controlling nature extended beyond just my finances. Every time I made a purchase, he would immediately call me, questioning my spending and demanding to know what I had bought. It became unbearable. Even something as simple as grocery shopping had turned into a distressing ordeal. To counter this, I started withdrawing cash during my grocery transactions. This way, my purchases would appear as regular expenses on the transaction records, preventing him from scrutinizing my spending habits.

It was a small act of defiance on my part, a way to reclaim some power over my own finances. During this period, I found myself relying on Ephedrine to stay awake. The unaddressed trauma from my past was draining me both physically and emotionally.

Oliver's relentless control knew no bounds. He wanted to know every minute detail about my consumption habits. He even went as far as calling the supplement stores and threatening them not to sell their products to me. His demands regarding having another baby continued incessantly. I resorted to faking a pregnancy just to get him off my back. All I wanted was for him to stop pestering me, and the lie seemed like a small price to pay.

Another reason behind the fabricated pregnancy was to test him to see if he would stick around. Looking back, I realize how immature that decision was.

Oliver became upset when I went for a run. He despised the idea, believing it was unsafe for me, given my condition. He wouldn't even allow me to go to the gym alone.

Things took an even darker turn when I tried to skip church on Sundays. He would become infuriated, disappointed that I couldn't meet his expectations.

And if things couldn't get any worse, Steven was taking me to court in Fort McMurray. Despite the fact that the children and I lived in Ontario, he had somehow managed to get out of jail. I'm still uncertain how he pulled it off. He even succeeded in hacking into my iCloud account, causing all his contacts to sync onto my phone. I knew he did it deliberately to upset me.

In contrast, during my court appearance, Oliver once again invaded my privacy by going through my phone, leading to another emotional breakdown triggered by an old text message. It felt as though fate was mocking me, especially when Steve fired his lawyer at the last minute, resulting in the court adjourning the case. Overwhelmed by Oliver's behavior, I decided to book a hotel room for my last night, hoping to escape the turmoil. However, something compelled me to check on Oliver that night. Against my better judgment, I entered the house and made my way to his bedroom. What I discovered was heart-wrenching – Oliver sitting on the bed, overwhelmed by sorrow, with a loaded gun in his mouth, prepared to end his pain.

Although I could have chosen to walk away, compassion tugged at my heartstrings. I stayed by his side, desperately trying to console him and offer the support that I myself had never received. In the following weeks, he traveled to Ottawa, providing me with an opportunity to share the news that I was no longer pregnant. As expected, the news hit him hard. Despite his emotional turmoil, he had gifted the children a Great Dane for Christmas, and we had all joyfully gone together to pick up the puppy. However, shortly after, when the kids were at school, and AL was asleep, Oliver started an argument, but I refused to engage. All I could do was run and seek refuge.

Descending the stairs, I sought solace in the depths of AB's closet, hiding in silence for what felt like an eternity. When I eventually emerged, I was greeted by an empty house. Every trace of Oliver, from the gifts he had purchased to the vehicle he had owned, had vanished. The moment the boys stepped off the bus, AB immediately inquired about the truck's whereabouts, and I had no choice but to break the devastating news that Oliver was gone.

The scream that erupted from AB still echoes in my ears to this day. All he had ever yearned for was a father who would never abandon him, and Oliver's departure shattered him. That piercing scream fueled my determination to ensure that no man would enter our lives again for the sake of my children. I was determined to break the cycle of abandonment.

Now burdened with stress, I found myself without a vehicle and insufficient finances to sustain the house we were living in. I felt lost and unsure of what to do. Then, out of the blue, my phone rang, and to my surprise, it was Steve offering a helping hand. Despite the restrictions placed upon our contact, he was willing to resolve my problems instantly. Renting me a vehicle and covering all my bills, I found myself unable to refuse his assistance, even though I should have been more cautious. How did he precisely know when to call and come to my rescue? Little did I know that everything was about to take a dark turn. On the morning of a deposition, I found myself driving to a supplement store, desperately seeking Ephedrine to combat my exhaustion. It was the only remedy that kept me awake and functioning. AL was with my parents while the boys accompanied me. I had to maintain my energy for their sake. Just as I was navigating the road, my phone rang, and Steve's voice filled the car through Bluetooth, allowing the kids to hear every word. However, I was not prepared for the verbal assault and threats that followed. I felt utterly humiliated as I caught a glimpse of myself in the rearview mirror, realizing that things were about to take a turn for the worse. Little did I know the extent of the impending ordeal.

Hurriedly parking at the supplement store, I was taken aback by the cold and distant attitude of the employee who had previously flirted with me. His colleagues, too, seemed unusually reserved. Leaving the store, I was suddenly surrounded by three police cars speeding towards us. My car was completely trapped. It was then that I realized they were there to arrest me, and the boys helplessly witnessed the distressing scene unfold before their eyes. The moment I laid eyes on the police, my PTSD kicked in, rendering me unable to comprehend or process anything or anyone around me. All I could hear were the anguished cries of my boys, who had not only heard the threatening phone call but were now experiencing this nightmare alongside me. At that moment, my sole focus was to protect my children and remove them from this harrowing situation. I pleaded desperately, but my pleas fell on deaf ears.

I can't help but feel that if the police had been educated about the signs and symptoms of PTSD, the situation could have been defused. Unfortunately, it seems that the Canadian police lack the necessary training and understanding when it comes to dealing with individuals who have mental or medical health issues. As a result, people like myself are left to face the consequences alone.

I found myself pleading with the police to take care of my children as they placed me in the back of the police car. All I wanted was to protect my kids and remove them from the chaotic situation. I didn't care about what would happen to me or what consequences I would face.

In my desperation, I started shouting and pounding on the doors, kicking the opposite door with my feet. I had completely lost control.

My instinct to protect my children, my mama bear spirit, took over. Their well-being became my sole focus, and I was determined to do whatever it took to ensure their safety. They had already been through so much, and I couldn't bear the thought of them witnessing their mother being arrested again.

I lay in the backseat, screaming for them to call my mother, my voice echoing like a broken record. Even though the doors remained closed, I kept shouting, and it felt like everyone had abandoned me. But I refused to abandon my children. Seeing them terrified only fueled my determination further. I continued to repeat my mother's phone number again and again, desperately hoping someone would listen.

"CALL MY MOM! CALL MY MOM!"

Those words became my desperate plea. Finally, an officer who had reached his limit approached me and made a deal - he would call my mom if I calmed down. I agreed without hesitation.

I said yes, and at last, he made the call and informed me that my mother was on her way. My children had already been taken to the police station for their safety. They drove me home and dropped me off, but my relief was short-lived. Steve's car, which he had rented me, had been towed.

Not only did I lose my car, but my driver's license was also revoked for three months, and I was charged with failure to comply. The situation was precarious, and I don't even remember being asked to take a breathalyzer test. It seemed like everything was stacked against me.

When you suffer from complex PTSD and find yourself triggered, it's as if you're transported to a different world, disconnected from reality. You relive past traumas, feeling completely detached from the present moment. Unfortunately, the police officers, as noted in their reports, misinterpreted my intentions and accused me of being confrontational. All I wanted was for them to listen, understand, and remove my kids from the danger. But they were unaware of my situation and lacked understanding.

People have reasons for their actions and who they are. "Be curious, not judgemental" - Walt Whitman. It's a principle I live by today. The officers also claimed that I smelled of alcohol, which may have been true since I had been drinking the night before. But, they failed to recognize that my erratic behavior was a result of being transported back to a traumatic experience, where I fought desperately for my life and the safety of my children. At that moment, it felt like I was trapped in a foggy bubble, locked in fight mode, where all I could hear and see were echoes of my past trauma. I wish the other officers had been trained in understanding PTSD. They could have intervened appropriately and de-escalated the situation instead of making it worse. They would have known the steps to bring me back to the present, and I would have cooperated willingly. It makes me wonder how many others with PTSD face similar crises and arrests without the necessary support and understanding.

I don't blame the officers, but I strongly believe that there needs to be a genuine reform in how they are trained to handle situations involving individuals with mental health issues. They need to approach each case with sensitivity and consideration for the individual's well-being.

Later that night, Steve called me, laughing, and asked how everything had turned out. He assured me that he had found the best criminal lawyer and had already retained him for me. He had planned it all. It was a calculated move.

On another occasion, I went out drinking while my mom stayed over at my place because my dad was in the hospital. No one knew about my outing. I took an Uber to the Fairmont, craving their soup and their aged-smoked whiskey - my favorite indulgences.

After a night at the strip club, where I drank more than usual, my phone started ringing incessantly. Reluctantly, I answered, only to be bombarded with questions from Steve's mother about my presence at the strip club. I hung up, refusing to engage further. The calls continued, but I refused to pick up. I met a few respectful gentlemen at the club who offered to drive me home. They didn't make any advances or inappropriate gestures. When I finally arrived home, I had no choice but to answer my phone. This time, it was Steve interrogating me about my visit to the Fairmont and the men who drove me home. I still don't understand how he knew about it, and perhaps I never will. It remains a mystery, but by then, nothing surprised me anymore.

During that time, AB had gone to stay with my parents. It still confuses me why my parents, to this day, show favoritism towards my oldest son, even though all three are their grandchildren. Less than a month after my arrest in early January 2019, I heard someone entering the house. To my horror, it was Steve.

He wasn't supposed to be around me due to his probation and conditions. Paranoia consumed me as I realized he had an uncanny ability to manipulate every situation to his advantage. The chilling control he exerted over the chain of events left me terrified.

I vividly recall the day my son, AJ, innocently alerted me, "Mommy, someone's at the door." Before I could react, Steve had already barged into our home. I stood frozen, staring at him, unsure of how to proceed. Panic coursed through my veins as I instinctively shielded AJ, urging him to leave. The situation was spiraling out of control.

But Steve's response was far from what I expected. He swiftly wrapped his hands around my neck, squeezing with an unimaginable force. Darkness enveloped me as I lost consciousness right in front of my children. When I awoke, I found myself cowering before him, obedient and submissive. I was trapped, with no escape except to comply with his every command. Sleep became a distant memory, especially when he was present. I had to adapt to his presence as he invaded our home for an extended period.

I suspected that he had come for AL's birthday, which fell on January 5th. The day finally arrived, and around 11:00, AJ rushed to inform me that there were police officers at our front door. Steve was still inside, and the news struck me dumb. Meanwhile, Steve scurried away, hiding while warning me not to say a word, accompanied by a dire threat. Fear gripped me as I realized he suspected me of calling the police. The reality of what he was capable of intensified my dread, and I needed to prove my innocence.

Summoning my courage, I opened the door to face the police officers standing outside. To my dismay, I discovered Oliver standing beside them. It turned out that Oliver had flown in to retrieve his remaining belongings, including his Harley Davidson, which he had left behind. The officers were there to accompany him. They proceeded to search AJ's room for the item Oliver sought.

Oliver pulled out a suitcase from the closet and placed it on the floor. It was no ordinary children's suitcase filled with clothes. As Oliver rummaged through it, he pulled out men's clothing, a shaving kit, and prescriptions with Steve's name on it. The room now contained Oliver, me, and the police. Sensing an opportunity, I began creating a scene, raising my voice and shouting as loudly as possible.

My hope was that my overreaction would prompt the officers to dig deeper to connect the dots. I longed for them to arrest me, convinced it would ensure the safety of both me and my children in police custody. It was a desperate plan formed on the spot.

However, they remained unmoved. I had to abandon my futile attempts and quietly confess the truth. I discreetly informed them that Steve was still inside the house. Even that move, in my opinion, would likely backfire eventually.

The officers simply instructed me to be quiet, sit down, and focus on my children. I could only do my best, dropping subtle hints along the way.

The presence of an unfamiliar Suburban in the garage, despite my suspended license, went unquestioned. The police were aware of it, yet they made no effort to investigate the plates or inquire about my access to the vehicle. As we descended into the basement, I caught sight of Steve sneaking out of the house like a shadow, making his way to the garage. He later confessed that he had hidden in the Suburban, lying flat on the floor to avoid detection.

I stood there with the officers and Oliver, watching as they inspected the Suburban through its windows. At that moment, I lost all hope. It was foolish to continue fighting. There was no point in trying to convince them any further. I fell silent and simply followed their lead. Eventually, they left, and the coast was clear. Steve called an Uber and departed. Shortly after that terrifying incident, I made the decision to move, finding a place of my own across the street from my parents, back in my hometown.

I had reached my breaking point. I was DONE! It was not safe for me to be away from people or anyone unfamiliar with my identity. However, there were some advantages to living in a small town where everyone knew everyone's business.

People were aware of my actions and even knew my schedule, such as when I would go to the gym. It was a predictable move, to say the least.

A few days before my relocation, I attended a party hosted by a girlfriend and met someone who offered to assist me with moving. I saw his kindness as a blessing and was genuinely grateful.

We rented a U-Haul, and he helped me pack up the first load. He drove the truck while I accompanied my dad. Unfortunately, since I didn't possess a driver's license, the U-Haul never made it to my new home.

It was later found empty and dropped off. I reported the incident, but it turned into a he-said-she-said situation. The police dismissed it as a civil matter, which left me disappointed. I understood their limitations and accepted that there was nothing more they could do.

Later on, I received a call from Steve, warning me that things would only worsen if I spoke up. Overwhelmed, I broke down in tears, pleading for him to leave me alone.

Everything I held dear was gone; the kids' toys, sentimental items like AB's cherished stuffed animals, and valuable possessions like designer shoes, clothes, and bags from Gucci, Louis Vuitton, and Christian Louboutin.

Everything that held value to me vanished in the blink of an eye. Experiencing the devastation of losing your prized possessions teaches you a profound, hard life lesson. It reminded me how much I invested my interest and love in materialism.

In the grand scheme of things, these are quite insignificant to me. I held them in high regard, not knowing they were temporary possessions. Still, the separation gave me a chance to introspect and reevaluate my attachment to physical objects.

At the end of the day, they are just things. They can always be replaced. What truly matters is the well-being and beautiful memories I made with my eternal children.

Looking back, I have undergone an incredible transformation both internally and externally in the past four years. It is a miraculous journey that few people can fully comprehend. My story remains unknown to others.

I don't look like what I've been through. No one has any idea the amount of dedication and perseverance it has taken to look at myself in the mirror day in and day out to finally get to where I am today. I look at myself in the mirror and love the woman looking right back at me.

When you come out of the storm, you won't be the same person who walked in. You will no longer fear the darkness, knowing the journey made you as bright as the sun.

Luke 8:17:

"Everything done in the dark will come to light."

Chapter 17: Breaking Free

So, my mom and I had this unspoken agreement. The plan was for AB to stay with her and my dad while I gave the new place a fresh coat of paint, unpacked, and got everything in order. But amidst the whirlwind of moving, I found myself caught in a reflective moment. "There has to be more to life than this," I mused.

Memories of a care package from a kind woman in the neighborhood resurfaced. Curious and a tad desperate, I rummaged through my things to find it. I was seeking answers. Why was life taking me through such a roller-coaster? This chaotic existence was not what I signed up for.

Steve, well, he was relentless. He wanted back in – not just in my life but in the kids' lives, too. I did my best, even facilitating the court-ordered FaceTime calls for the children. But the man had a penchant for pain; he seemed to derive some twisted pleasure from it.

One day, out of the blue, he decided to fill me in, in graphic detail no less, about how he'd slept with several girls from my nursing program. These were young girls, barely adults, some of whom I'd hosted for dinner. His confession was a calculated attack, and it tore me apart.

However, karma did come around, even if it was brief. Steve got arrested again for breaching his conditions. But the law, with its loopholes, only gave him more conditions – a mere slap on the wrist, really. And Steve, being Steve, treated these legal bindings like a game, dancing between them with a sly grin.

He had a manipulative grip over me, this dark, shadowy power. Whenever I mustered the strength to stand up for myself, there was always a price to pay. He was the puppet master, his life an intricate web of lies, and I was often caught in the crosshairs.

The constant anxiety, always being on the edge, took its toll on me. I started losing my hair. Until one day, my reflection showed a bald head. And my voice? Gone for four excruciating years. Living in a state of high alert, 24/7, was slowly but surely breaking me.

I was drowning in *waves of depression*. It felt like I was operating on autopilot, doing just enough to scrape by, perpetually stuck in survival mode — fight or flight, every second of the day. My primary focus was showing up for the kids, even when it felt impossible. In the midst of this emotional chaos, I had to somehow gather the strength to heal while also complying with the court orders. Steve was granted FaceTime rights with the kids, a directive which he twisted to his advantage. He was allowed four calls a week, scheduled at 6:00 p.m. Eastern Standard Time. But he didn't stick to the timetable. He'd call at random times, using work as an excuse. And when I couldn't answer, he'd manipulate the situation, pushing the blame on me. He'd lace his words with guilt, making me feel ashamed for "violating" court orders.

Bit by bit, I found myself bending to his whims once more. He wormed his way back into my life, cunningly making me feel financially dependent on him. In his twisted narrative, he was always the victim, and I was painted as the problem.

The waves of mental and emotional abuse didn't stop with me; they spilled over onto the kids. He'd engage in a sinister dance of breadcrumbing – popping into their lives with promises, raising their hopes, only to vanish and start the cycle again. The inconsistency took a heavy toll on the children's mental health. When he sent e-transfers, he'd hold back the password, using it as a carrot to make me dance to his tune.

Amidst this storm, I was desperately trying to heal. I quit smoking, stayed sober, and refrained from drugs. The challenge was finding a way to clear my mind. *How do I find clarity amidst all this chaos?* Then, one sweltering summer day, the weight of my financial struggles bore down on me. Steve, seizing an opportunity, called. He tried to blackmail me, coercing me into letting him see the kids. His influence was suffocating — the way he'd oscillate between moments of feigned affection and intense devaluation. It was a tumultuous mental rollercoaster. The resulting emotional turbulence clouded my mind, leaving me lost in a thick fog, bereft of clarity.

One evening, he called me up, his voice dripping with faux sweetness, insisting I meet him at a nearby hotel. He dangled the bait – a replacement for my stolen Louis Vuitton, my favorite one, stuffed with $10,000 cash. The catch? I just had to bring the kids.

He manipulated my sense of self-worth to the point where it felt like I was deserving of the pain. My brain grappled with the disparity between the man I thought he was and the monster he revealed himself to be. This internal battle tore me apart, deepening my confusion. Naively, I clung to hope, blinded by the desire for change. My unwavering loyalty and the kindness I harbored became his carte blanche to abuse me relentlessly. The torment began to affect my children, too. To outsiders who casually say, "Just leave," they can't fathom the crippling weight of that decision. Especially when you feel isolated, without an ally to turn to, driven by desperation, I took the kids to meet him in Quebec. He chose the location meticulously; Quebec's detachment from the other Canadian police departments provided him a haven. Leaving the kids alone with him wasn't an option. He flew into Ottawa, and we endured a nightmarish 48 hours at the Hilton. While he lavished the children with extravagant gifts – plush wardrobes, high-end gadgets, and the like – the emotional toll of the stay was catastrophic. Every ounce of healing and progress I'd achieved was eviscerated. I found myself plummeting back into the darkest pits of despair. During our stay, he announced he had to leave urgently due to his father's alleged near-death condition in the hospital. Although upset, the kids and I empathized with his situation. But this also gave me a respite from his malevolence.

However, his deceit was boundless. For reasons unknown, a gut instinct nudged me to verify the news with his father directly. When I reached out, his father was perfectly healthy. The realization struck like lightning – that was the final straw. The last time I would endure his treachery.

In the aftermath, I spiraled into a realm of despair few could comprehend. Alone with my torment, I found solace in the numbing embrace of alcohol. For two grueling months, I drowned my sorrows in daily doses of vodka. And while it's inconceivable that those around me remained oblivious to my downfall, not a soul intervened. This further eroded my trust, pushing me to avoid everyone and everything.

Chapter 18: Silence Is Not Golden

Living with PTSD is absolutely debilitating. The intrusive thoughts bombard my mind throughout the day, and relentless flashbacks assault my senses - the smell of gasoline, the taste of vodka, the feeling of his fists, and the sight of his rage contort my body and mind into uncontrollable reactions.

Irritability and mood swings possess me without warning. I startle so easily that the slightest sound makes me jump out of my skin. You have to gently announce yourself before entering a room, no sudden moves, or I just might lash out in fear of being attacked. The kids know not to scare me or pop up unexpectedly beside my bed at night. They must declare their presence like royalty to avoid triggering me.

The nightmares never cease. I wake up panicking, feeling my head to ensure my hair and skin haven't melted off as they did in the dream, where Steve doused me with gasoline and lit the match. The kids find me frantically patting my body to verify that the nightmare was just a cruel illusion.

One horrific day, I sent the kids to my parents' house. In the basement, I wrapped a hot pink extension cord around the rafters. Upstairs in the laundry room, I sat staring at a 1.75-liter bottle of vodka. I twisted off the cap and started chugging, determined to down the entire bottle. Gripping the cord in one hand, visions of ending my insufferable life once and for all consumed me. I couldn't take the pain for another second. This was it - I had reached the lowest point imaginable and saw no way out. Something inexplicable came over me and guided me up the stairs. I stumbled across the street and collapsed at my parents' kitchen table, weeping uncontrollably. I begged them, "Take me to the hospital now. I need help right now." That marked the first day of the rest of my life. I can't fully explain what happened, but I know some force turned me around when I was completely resolved to hang myself that day.

I detoxed in the hospital psychiatric ward and voluntarily surrendered my license until I healed. Checking myself into the Royal Ottawa Mental Health Centre, I stayed with my parents for three months before feeling strong enough to go back home with the kids.

One day, my mom harshly scolded me for not being "stronger than this," her words cut deep as she judged me in front of the children. In my fragile state, my parents dragged me to a lawyer's office to sign away temporary custody "for the kids' safety" in case my ex tried to take them. Little did I know this document would later be used to keep my son from me indefinitely. I was far too psychologically unstable to grasp the implications of signing away my rights as their mother. You should be able to trust your own parents, but I had no idea they would eventually forbid me from seeing my son or obtaining any information about him. The wound cuts deeper with each passing day.

No one sees the battles I wage within, the silent struggles that have carved my path to where I stand today. Each step forward has been a result of the quiet, unwavering work I've undertaken, often in solitude. Transforming pain into healing without lashing out at those around me has been my strength. During my stay at the Royal Ottawa, whispers among the nurses and physicians about a transformative book caught my attention. *The Body Keeps the Score* by Bessel van der Kolk. Eager for change, I delved into its pages, absorbing knowledge and, soon enough, crafting a plan for my own healing journey. Fifteen years, I'd been on antidepressants. Armed with newfound insights from the book, I approached my doctor about combining Zoloft with EMDR—a therapy showing promise in alleviating PTSD symptoms.

After wrapping up my time at Royal Ottawa, I threw myself wholeheartedly into virtual EMDR sessions. I was unrelenting in my quest for self-betterment, seeking knowledge and understanding about my own psyche. The shadow work was grueling—confronting every past mistake and dissecting every decision that brought me to my present. Yet, I persisted. Nightly sleep affirmations became my balm, reprogramming deep-seated beliefs and behaviors. Coupled with daily meditation and personal affirmations, I gradually rebuilt my subconscious mind.

For over two years, I maintained an unwavering routine—rising at 4:00 a.m., dedicating the first three hours of dawn to self-care. This rigorous discipline stemmed from a profound love for myself. My immersion in the Bible, questioning its teachings and seeking answers, taught me a valuable lesson: Everyone has a unique story and relationship with God. *How you nurture that bond is personal.*

All one needs is the openness to ask and the willingness to receive. Over time, you build trust with God, learning to navigate life with unwavering faith. As Matthew 7:7-8 eloquently puts it, "Ask, and it will be given to you. Seek, and you will find. Knock, and the door will be opened to you. For everyone who asks receives, and the one who seeks finds. And to the one who knocks, the door will be opened." Throughout this unpredictable, tumultuous journey, one truth has become crystal clear to me: You can't enforce your beliefs, values, or religious inclinations onto someone else. It's like trying to mold clay that's already set—impossible and futile. Instead, it's more fulfilling to serve as a gentle guide, subtly illuminating the path and allowing others to find their way in their own time.

The words of Psalm 119:105 resonate deeply within me, "Your word is a lamp to my feet and a light to my path." It's an affirmation that there's always light, even in the darkest corners of our journey.

Around a year after I embarked on my rigorous journey of self-healing and discovery, my mother slid a document across the table with an air of unsettling calmness. A document she had carefully drafted sought to declare that I had custody of only two of my children while AB, my precious son, would be under the sole custody of my parents. This wasn't a mere piece of paper. It felt like chains attempting to shackle me to a past I was desperate to move beyond.

My internal alarm system went into overdrive—*What the fuck is happening?* Trying to keep the whirlwind of emotions from showing on my face, I firmly, yet calmly, rejected her proposition. "Absolutely not." Her mounting agitation was directly proportional to my growing resolve. As her frustrations flared, my intuition, that inner voice that had been subdued for so long, began shouting louder, warning me of an impending storm. And true to my intuition's warning, a year later, that document made an unwelcome reappearance at the school office. But now, it bore the scars of tampering—an added paragraph, a forged signature. My mother's attempt at manipulation was glaringly evident. The pain was immediate and intense, like an arrow piercing straight through my heart. But, drawing upon my newfound resilience, I managed to keep my exterior calm. I requested a copy of the document and continued with the rest of the day's obligations, letting the pain wash over me like a silent tidal wave.

Once the hustle and bustle of the day, the duties of motherhood, and the routine chores all ebbed away, I allowed myself a moment of vulnerability. Alone in my sanctuary, the gravity of the betrayal hit me. But amid the pain was a revelation—this incident, as devastating as it was, was also proof of my journey of self-growth. The older, unhealed version of me might have retaliated with unchecked rage. But now, my response was instinctive and calm. A realization dawned on me: *I've truly metamorphosed.*

The reactions from those who've been an integral part of my life were starkly clear. They were resistant, even hostile, to this evolved version of myself. Time and again, they sought to prod and provoke, trying to drag me back into a whirlpool of past mistakes and regrets. Their taunts and actions were attempts to keep me ensnared in my history. However, I realized it wasn't just about me—it was also about them. They used my past as a smokescreen to hide from their own imperfections.

The anguish of being willfully separated from one's child, especially when orchestrated by someone you once revered, is ineffable. I reached out multiple times, yearning for those fleeting moments of joy—sharing a simple meal with my son, having him stay overnight at my place, and building memories together.

But every plea was met with cold denial. Instead of letting him savor the carefree joys of childhood, they bound him in premature responsibilities—making him work on weekends, during snow days, and even pulling him out of school for work commitments.

Their influential standing in the community muzzled my protests. Their attempts to silence me were relentless, from wielding their social status like a weapon to threatening legal repercussions if I dared voice my concerns.

However, amid all this turmoil, I found a new perspective. I could either succumb to their manipulation or use it as fuel for my journey of self-improvement. So, while they remained obsessed with pulling me down, I was firmly focused on rising, evolving, and becoming the best version of myself. I was no longer willing to be a pawn in their game.

The oppressive weight of silence, the iron shackles of fear, were wielded against me, using them as instruments to keep me and my children subdued. Yet, in this whirlpool of emotions, there's not an ounce of shame in my heart for the trials I've endured. Rather, I've come to realize that silence is the great enabler, the unsung accomplice that lets abuse perpetuate.

It's an exhausting feat, trying to reason with those who are blinded by their own versions of the truth. Their perceptions, clouded by ego, bitterness, and deep-seated resentment, make them impervious to logic. No matter the weight of evidence or the clarity of argument, their minds are impenetrable fortresses, barricaded against all but their own skewed beliefs. It became evident that they were not seeking truth but validation for their prejudiced viewpoints. And so, I learned a valuable lesson—when ignorance chooses to bellow, intelligence whispers. The peace I've meticulously crafted, the serenity I've won after years of internal warfare, is now my most treasured possession.

Every day, I'm reminded of AB's absence. It's a piercing pain, a constant sting. But I've made it a ritual, a solemn promise to myself and to him, to walk my children to school. Twice daily, I walk my two younger children and, later, my oldest son. Rain or shine, I stand outside, waiting. It's more than just a walk; it's a testament. A silent declaration that no matter the distance, no matter the barriers placed between us, he will always find me there, ready to guide, support, and love him.

The same shadows of my tumultuous past now threaten my son. It's a haunting déjà vu, watching history repeat itself, only this time, it's not just about me—it's about my child.

My parents have become artists of deception, painting an image of me that's far from reality. Yet, deep down, I know that their canvas of lies will never eclipse the genuine, resilient spirit standing defiantly in their presence.

The adversities I face, I've come to understand, are not punishments; they're lessons, molding and refining me. When detractors fail to taint the person I've become, they desperately dig, attempting to resurrect the ghosts of my past.

But their efforts are in vain. This transformative journey, every tear, every revelation, every epiphany, has been diligently documented. Flipping through the pages of my journal, the person from a year, even six months ago, feels like a distant memory, a stranger. It fills me with gratitude and profound pride in the mountains I've scaled and the valleys I've traversed. Through introspection, I've realized that our harshest judgments are often reflections of our internal struggles. Every time I found myself envious of someone else's life, their appearance, or material possessions, it was an indication of the facets of myself I was uncomfortable with or those I yearned for. It wasn't them; it was the battle within me.

The power of self-awareness is transformative, a realization that acts as a compass in the storm of life. Our ego, with its myriad facets, brings forth the duality in our consciousness. The ethereal words echo in my mind, *"In unity, the soul answered, I saw you. You did not see me, nor did you know me. You mistook the garment I wore for my true self, and you did not recognize me."* A reflection from Mary nine, verses four through six, from the Gospel of Mary Magdalene.

Through a journey marked by trials and tribulations, I've painfully discerned there's no circumventing the process. You can't side-step it. You can't duck beneath it, nor can you leap over. The only path is right through the heart of it. It demands you to confront those agonizing, uneasy emotions, those memories that send shivers down your spine. You're compelled to analyze them. *Why do you feel this way? What is its root?*

It's only when you immerse yourself, allowing the waves of these emotions to crash over you, that you find clarity. Once you've traversed this harrowing path, the burdens that once seemed impossible become stepping stones, forging you into a stronger version of yourself. It's an arduous process, delving deep into one painful memory after another, but with each conquest, the chains of the past become weaker.

"Why," I frequently pondered, "Do the same calamities befall me, each time more ferocious than the last?" I experienced a revelation that maybe, just maybe, if I altered my perspective and sought a different approach, I could transcend these relentless mountains of anguish. It's a journey inward, where you cease seeking validation from the world, relying solely on the wisdom of your own soul. It's a profound realization that all the tools, all the strength you've ever required, reside within you.

The epiphany dawns like the first light of dawn. The tumultuous roller coaster of trauma, heartbreak, addiction, and suffering halts. Not because it ran its course but because you chose to disembark, confronting your demons head-on. What was once a chaotic descent transforms into the wheel of fortune, spinning ever in your favor.

Amidst life's turmoil, you come to discern that while external factors are beyond your grasp, your inner world is your dominion. The deeper you journey within, the more tranquil the waters become. The chaos of manipulation, deceit, and external control fades away, replaced by a serene flow of living in the present. As you inch closer to your genuine self, external disturbances diminish. Your reality becomes a canvas painted with your aspirations and dreams.

To those from my past who wronged me, I bear no grudges. My heart brims with forgiveness and love for each of them. Even for my ex-husband, despite the torment he put me through, I harbor no resentment. Many have remarked *it's unusual for someone to still have affection after such betrayal.* But my choice is simple: Love over hate. Refusing to let my past cast a shadow over my future, I've chosen warmth over coldness, love over bitterness. My capacity to forgive and to love unconditionally might be viewed as a flaw by many, including my own father. But it's this very trait, this boundless heart, that I believe draws God closer to me.

Today, as I stand here, over a year has elapsed since I've forsaken all medications. The dark specter of my PTSD hasn't shown itself. Pride surges through me as I reflect on the woman I've morphed into. Overcoming hurdles many stumble upon, there's but one entity I owe it to: The unending grace of God.